Praise for Books from Plar

T0273189

The Sh*t's Hit the Fan ... Now What?!

In this latest book Rhonda Abrams has confirmed once again why she is a respected thought leader on what makes small businesses work. Her passion, dedication, and commitment to helping businesses achieve success is evident in all that she does. Whether you are a startup, a mature business, or someone who supports them—this book is essential reading to give you the knowledge, tools, and inspiration that you need to succeed.

—Isaac D. Kremer, Executive Director,
Metuchen Downtown Alliance, Metuchen, New Jersey

Rhonda Abrams is a brilliant and impassioned advocate for American small business. When my friends and family's businesses were floundering to survive the pandemic, Rhonda's amazing podcast series covering the governments' loan programs, including Paycheck Protection Program (PPP), was a lifesaver...She quickly became our top source of information. Through her counsel several friends and family members received business-saving assistance. We can't thank Rhonda enough!

—M. Davis, Atlanta, GA

Rhonda Abrams is 100% by our side AND on our side through the challenges and blessings of developing small business viability and sustainability. For America's Small Business Development Counselors, Rhonda's insight, articles, and no-nonsense actionable advice are priceless elements to share with our clients and our SBDC Team...She is hands-on, accessible, and brilliant in diagnosing countless small business issues...and presenting practical, imaginative solutions.

—Rita Mitchell, USM Small Business Development Center

Shortly after a Shelter-in-Place order was issued in Palm Springs, my husband & business partner and I were so lost as to what was happening...Rhonda was a beacon of light and hope in helping guide us thru the unprecedented times...By closely following Rhonda in March, April and May—I was able to apply early on for both the EIDL and PPP loans...I am so grateful I was connected with Rhonda in such an uncertain time.

—Brandon Lindley, co-owner, Havaianas, Palm Springs, CA

Successful Business Plan: Secrets & Strategies

"[*Successful Business Plan*] is user-friendly and exhaustive...highly recommended. Abrams' book works because she tirelessly researched the subject. Most how-to books on entrepreneurship aren't worth a dime; among the thousands of small business titles, Abrams' [is an] exception."

— *Forbes Magazine*

"There are plenty of decent business-plan guides out there, but Abrams' was a cut above the others I saw. *Successful Business Plan* won points with me because it was thorough and well organized, with handy worksheets and good quotes. Also, Abrams does a better job than most at explaining the business plan as a planning tool rather than a formulaic exercise. Well done."

— *Inc. Magazine*

Six-Week Startup

"What I love about Rhonda Abrams' new edition of her bestselling book *Six-Week Startup* is that it focuses on action. So many people that want to start businesses never actually get it off the ground. Rhonda's book gives a step-by-step approach to launching your new company, including licenses, branding, setting up your office, marketing, money plus easy-to-use checklists and worksheets."

— *Barry Moltz, Small business expert, author and radio show host*

Business Plan In A Day

"A business plan is something every business needs, but too many fail to create one because it seems intimidating. Rhonda Abrams is on a mission to change that. With this book she shows you how to create a professional business plan that will seem like it took weeks to write instead of 24 hours."

— *Anita Campbell, Publisher of Small Business Trends*

Actual ratings and quotes from online reviews at Amazon

Successful Business Plan: Secrets & Strategies

Buy it now or miss a plethora of very useful knowledge

Quite possibly the best book out there to give your plan the momentum to get it done and get it right! This book is worth more than its weight in gold. I was intimidated at first glance, but the content flows seamlessly and the worksheets are a fantastic planning tool, some of them can even be physical pieces of the business plan. I highly recommend to anyone serious about starting a business, get this book immediately, regardless of where you are at in your planning process and you'll be the next person writing a 5 star review. Get it done and get it right!

Jam Packed with Secrets and Strategies—Don't Pass This Book Up!

Ms. Abrams has done an excellent job of putting it all together and imparting concrete business wisdom. The book is up-to-date and a great resource for anyone in business be it a small or large business. She hit the nail on the head in the Financial section. She is correct in strongly asserted that you DON'T ignore your finances if you're having a bad month. I wish I had been taught from this book when I was in College!

Six-Week Startup: A Step-by-Step Program for Starting your Business, Making Money, and Achieving your Goals

I started...and opened in six-weeks!

This is a great book for business beginners (and even those who are on their second or third time around). It walks you through the well suggested steps of getting started. If you follow the plan...you should realistically be able to "start" in 6-weeks.

Very helpful

This book really does what it promises. I went through each week/chapter writing down what Rhonda told me to. It all flowed together beautifully, and I am now almost ready to put my web site live and ready for sales. I also contacted SCORE and the SBA as per her recommendation, and have the added value of the counsel of hundreds of counselors who can speak specifically into my situation. I don't think there is anything else Rhonda could add to make this book a better choice for the virgin entrepeneur. Four thumbs up—two are from my SBA counselor!

Entrepreneurship: A Real-World Approach

You CAN be an entrepreneur!

This second edition of what was a good book to begin with has made enough changes to make it an excellent guide for those thinking about starting their own business. It begins with exploring what it means to be an entrepreneur, moves into and provides tools and strategies for developing and planning a business, takes the next step to create the internal operational framework to meet the needs of all stakeholders in the business, and then ends with some suggestions on how to grow the business even into a global market. Being filled with outstanding examples and scenarios, the book is easy to read, follow, and understand. There are pages of references, extra sources, and practical applications that will guide nearly every business idea into a potentially thriving enterprise. The price of the book is a bargain considering the wealth that is in its pages.

Great Book for Beginners

Great book insight and provides sections as to where to begin. Includes chapters on marketing, legal, naming your business and more. Great book!

The
SH*T's
hit the fan...

NOW
WHAT?!

99 Recession-Proof Tips
FOR SMALL BUSINESS SUCCESS

by Rhonda Abrams

PlanningShop™
Palo Alto, California

The SH*T'S Hit the Fan: Now What?!
© 2020 by Rhonda Abrams
Published by PlanningShop™

Services for our readers:

Colleges, business schools, corporate purchasing:

PlanningShop™ offers special discounts and supplemental teaching materials for universities, business schools, and corporate training.

Contact: info@planningshop.com or call 650-364-9120 Monday-Friday 9 am - 5 pm PST.

Free business tips and information:
To receive PlanningShop's free email newsletter on starting and growing a successful business, sign up at www.PlanningShop.com.

> PlanningShop
> 555 Bryant Street, #180
> Palo Alto, CA 94301 USA
> 650-364-9120
>
> Fax: 650-364-9125
> Email: info@PlanningShop.com
> www.PlanningShop.com

PlanningShop™ is a division of Rhonda, Inc., a California corporation.

Editor: Anne Marie Bonneau
Copyeditor: Emily Pickard
Cover and Interior Design: Diana Russell, DianaRussellDesign.com

978-1-933895-91-8 (eBook)
978-1-933895-92-5 (Trade)
Library of Congress Control Number: 2020946105

"This publication is designed to provide accurate and authoritative information in regard to the subject matter covered. It is sold with the understanding that the publisher and author are not engaged in rendering legal, accounting, or other professional services. If legal advice or other expert assistance is required, the services of a competent professional person should be sought."

> — *from a Declaration of Principles jointly adopted by a committee of the American Bar Association and a committee of publishers*

About Rhonda Abrams

 Entrepreneur, author, and nationally syndicated columnist Rhonda Abrams is widely recognized as one of the leading experts on entrepreneurship and small business. Rhonda's column for *USA Today* is the most widely distributed column on small business and entrepreneurship in the United States, reaching tens of millions of readers. She was named one of the "Top 30 Global Gurus" for Startups.

Rhonda's books have been used by millions of entrepreneurs. Her first book, *Successful Business Plan: Secrets & Strategies*, is the best-selling business plan guide in America and has sold over 2 million copies. It was named one of the Top Ten business books for entrepreneurs by both *Forbes* and *Inc.* magazines, and one of the 100 best business strategy books of all time. Rhonda's other books are perennial best-sellers, with three of them having reached the nationally recognized "Top 50 Business Bestseller" list.

Rhonda not only writes about business—she lives it! As the founder of three successful companies, Rhonda has accumulated an extraordinary depth of experience and a real-life understanding of the challenges facing entrepreneurs. Rhonda first founded a management consulting practice working with clients ranging from one-person startups to Fortune 500 companies. Rhonda was an early online pioneer, founding a website for small business that she later sold. In 1999, Rhonda started a publishing company—now called PlanningShop—focusing exclusively on topics of business planning, entrepreneurship, and new business development. PlanningShop is America's leading academic publisher focusing exclusively on entrepreneurship.

A popular public speaker, Rhonda is regularly invited to address leading industry and trade associations, business schools, and corporate conventions and events. Educated at Harvard University and UCLA, where she was named Outstanding Senior, Rhonda lives in Palo Alto, California.

 facebook.com/RhondaAbramsSmallBusiness

 twitter.com/RhondaAbrams

 instagram.com/rhondaabrams

NOW WHAT?! Contents

THE SH*T'S HIT THE FAN ...

NOW WHAT?!

99 RECESSION-PROOF TIPS FOR SMALL BUSINESS SUCCESS

GET YOUR HEAD IN THE GAME

Let's face it: the proverbial sh*t's hit the fan

Yes, that language is a bit crude, but what else can you say when, in response to a worldwide pandemic, the entire economy came to a screeching halt? When business as we knew it changed virtually overnight?

If you run a business—or want to start a business—you've never been faced with anything like this. Even the Great Depression—another worldwide economic catastrophe—didn't happen as dramatically, as quickly, as the economic impact of Covid-19. Small businesses, in particular, are challenged by this new reality and startups face unchartered waters.

Whether you're an existing business, a startup, or hope to launch a company, you're dealing with challenges few entrepreneurs have had to ever deal with before. But can challenging times lead to successful companies? Can what you're facing today lead you to survival, success, tomorrow?

We believe so—we know so. And we are here to help, with specific, time-tested do-it-now tips. In the pages that follow, we'll give you 99 specific things you can do now to help you survive and succeed—tips based on decades of experience with successful entrepreneurs—who've faced tough times and come out better on the other side. They could do it—and we believe so can you!

But to do so, you've got to have an attitude that success is possible. You have to be willing to change, to try new things, to fail. That's probably not hard for you—after all, you started (or are starting) a business. That means you already are the kind of person who can optimistically take risks.

So the first thing is to bring back that resilience, that can-do attitude that you already have. You've got to get your head in the game.

NOW WHAT?!

1. Think of yourself as a startup

Given the new reality—that you have to be nimble, change to meet new conditions, seize opportunities, work harder and longer than you have in years—it's helpful to think of yourself as a startup.

Yes, it's a useful mental exercise to shift your thinking to that of a startup mentality whether your business, indeed, is just getting off the ground, or if you've been in business for years, even decades. In a recession—in a vastly changing economy and society—no matter how long you've been in business, you are actually starting fresh, anew.

If you are actually just starting a business, there's a good chance that you have to veer away from your original concept, change your business model, even dramatically change the kinds of goods or services you thought you were going to offer. That's OK—most startups have to change course early on, regardless of economic conditions. Learn about some of those in the next tip.

For existing businesses, it may be more challenging to think of yourself as a startup since you've been at this for awhile—but it's a good way to approach running your company right now. Of course, you probably have some baggage that real startups don't have: leases, bills, inventory, employees, and more. But you also have a wealth of resources startups don't have: loyal customers, vendor relations, experienced employees, industry knowledge, contacts.

Embracing the idea of being a startup gives you more energy and a more positive outlook. Like a startup, you'll learn lots of new things. That's a good thing. The way your business—and yourself—will thrive, not just survive, is by growing in new directions. You will learn new ways of doing business, new things about your customers and potential customers, new ways that your industry is improving, new ways to manage money and manage people.

Sure, like a startup, you'll have to work hard, change fast, experience some setbacks, and money will be tight. But try to remember the optimism that someone starting a new business has—and, if you can, try to embody it yourself.

So think of yourself as a smart, experienced, hard-working startup. Let that experience and knowledge guide you—not handicap you—as you launch the next phase of your business.

STAY SANE!
TAKE HEART: THE ECONOMY WILL CHANGE

Whatever situation you are in now, sooner or later, it's going to change. The overall economic situation goes through cycles. Eventually economic conditions improve. History proves that the American economy—like the Canadian, European, and much of the rest of the world's economies—is resilient. You can be resilient too.

2. Stay agile, move fast

Businesses that survive are businesses that can change. Think about being mentally agile in your business the same way you think about being flexible—agile—in your body. If you just sit in the same position—never flexing your muscles, never exercising—you get stiff, old. If you want to survive both the current situation and thrive for the long-term, you've got to stay flexible in terms of your own attitude.

That's right—*attitude.* The single most important thing in preparing your business to survive in challenging economic times is your **attitude.** That may sound a bit simplistic, but it's true.

In good times—when your business may take a lot of work but not a lot of thought—you can often avoid changing. After all, things are rolling along smoothly.

In challenging economic times—when your business is under threat—you have to be willing to change, to try new things, to stretch your definition of how you see yourself. There's always a reason to do nothing, but if you want your small business to survive, doing nothing is not an option.

Think of this as your "spaghetti year"—throwing a lot of things against the wall to see what sticks. That means you have to be willing to try a bunch of new things. Some—many—of them will fail. You can't let that define or defeat you.

The key is to understand that changing is part of the process of surviving. When you see a need to change or opportunity to grow, move quickly. You can take charge of your own destiny—as much as you can—or you can let outside forces determine your future. A positive, flexible attitude certainly does not guarantee success. But in recessionary times, a negative, do-nothing attitude almost certainly guarantees failure.

The beginning of succeeding in a recession is to recognize you are going to have to change, you will sometimes fail, you will often be discouraged. But your own belief in yourself and your ability to tackle new situations will help you survive and succeed.

NOW WHAT?!

3. Be willing and able to "pivot"

It's worth repeating: "Pivot" is one of the words you're going to hear frequently in a challenging economy. With market transformations coming at us as rapidly as meteors, it's not at all surprising that you might be in one type of business—or have some business offerings—and now find yourself needing to change to—to pivot—to another.

You may find yourself pivoting because:

■ What you're doing is not working—it's time for "Plan B" and then "Plan C"

■ The changing business landscape presents opportunities and you want to seize those opportunities

■ One part of your business takes off, and you want to lean in to that growth opportunity

■ Your market is rapidly changing

■ Your industry is rapidly changing, particularly due to technological change

■ Economic, health, regulatory, or other external issues force you to change

■ Something better comes along

And, of course, we've seen how Covid-19 caused a massive need for change in how most small businesses do business.

When the world changes—as it has been doing lately—that creates new needs, and needs create opportunities. Many of the best pivots are inspired by a smart entrepreneur seeing—and seizing—an opportunity, particularly in their industry or area of expertise, often because they see a problem needing to be solved.

Pivoting is far more common than you'd ever imagine. Many of today's most successful companies started with a different concept, then changed when they hit a wall. Some well-known pivots include:

- ■ **Twitter** (www.twitter.com): a podcast directory called Odeo

- ■ **Pinterest** (www.pinterest.com): a mobile shopping site called Tote

- ■ **Instagram** (www.instagram.com): a social check-in site called Burbn

- ■ **PayPal** (www.paypal.com): a system to beam payments to Palm Pilots

One of the most successful pivots happened over a century ago. In 1902, five businessmen formed the Minnesota Mining and Manufacturing (MMM) company, bought a mine, and set out to extract a valuable mineral, corundum. Only problem: There was no corundum there. Whoops. The company quickly pivoted. The company now known as 3M (www.3m.com) started selling sandpaper (there was a lot of sand in that mine). But the company kept failing, and pivoting. Their openness eventually led 3M to become one of the world's most innovative companies. Some of the many inventions from 3M include masking tape, cellophane (scotch) tape, video tape, Post-it Notes, and a whole host of medical, solar, photographic, and industrial products.

Occasionally, business owners pivot because something better just comes along and presents itself. That requires an openness to change and a willingness to stretch yourself. That stretch may be a little—or it may be a lot.

For example, during the closure of restaurants caused by Covid-19, many restaurants "pivoted" to begin providing take-out meals, even if they'd never done that before. That was a first, and relatively easy, step for most. But some restaurant owners also found other sources of new revenue, such as selling meal kits, grocery items, conducting online cooking classes. Some went even farther. For example, a small chain of ice cream stores in Seattle—which made its own ice cream—was suddenly and completely closed at the beginning of the pandemic. The owner laid off virtually her entire staff, and things looked bleak. But she pivoted. Since her stores were closed, she started packaging and selling her ice cream to grocery stores. In doing so, she actually added a new line of business for her company— one that lasted after she was able to reopen her stores. That pivot helped her not only survive in the short run, but grow substantially.

4. Take advantage of the advantages of a down economy

While a down economy may seem like a tough time to launch, run, or grow a business, history has proven that many great businesses have started, survived, and expanded during troubled times.

Yes, it is certainly easier to launch, grow, or succeed in business in a strong and healthy economy when customers feel flush, profits are easier to achieve, you have more room to make mistakes and time to recover.

But here's the good news—history has shown that challenging economic conditions also create opportunities. Many successful businesses that are now household names actually started in recessions, the Great Depression, or in other down markets—just to name a few: General Electric, IBM, General Motors, Disney, Burger King, Microsoft, CNN, Apple, WhatsApp, Venmo, Uber, Square, Hewlett-Packard, Hyatt, Trader Joe's, FedEx, Electronic Arts, Airbnb. Wow! That's a lot of terrific companies that started during hard economic times.

In fact, a 2009 study by the reputable Kauffman Foundation found that more than half the companies in the Fortune 500 at that time were started during recessions or bear markets.

Why? How can a bad economy be a good time to start or grow a business?

■ **Customers are more open to change.** In good times, customers can afford to stick with current vendors and providers, often overlooking products or services that have slipped in quality, prices that have crept up, customer service that has lagged. When everything is in flux, customers re-evaluate previous purchasing decisions.

■ **Customers seek new, often less expensive, ways to meet their needs.** Cash-conscious customers look for ways to save money. They're willing to sacrifice some bells-and-whistles in their choice of providers as long as they find a viable alternative.

■ **Customers have new needs.** Changing societal and economic conditions often mean customers' situations have changed. They look for new products and services to meet their new needs. This is especially true in a society that has been so radically changed by recent events.

■ **Competitors may have higher fixed costs.** Long-established competitors may have high overhead: rent, equipment leases, long-term debt. That makes it difficult for them to reduce their prices to compete head-on with you.

■ **Competitors reduce their marketing.** Typically, one of the first things many companies do in a downturn is to cut their marketing and communication budgets. That creates an opening for you to aggressively market to prospects.

■ **Competitors are weakened or discouraged.** In a recession, many business owners and executives decide to stop, sell, or just get tired. Their inability or unwillingness to adapt to the new reality creates significant opportunities for you, if you're willing to step up now.

And, wait, there's more...It's not just that a down economy presents new opportunities; starting or running a business during recessionary times actually provides a few advantages over starting in high growth times. These include:

■ **Lower costs.** Generally, in a recession, prices for many critical business needs go down. You may be able to find less expensive rent, lower costs for raw material and inventory, reduced cost on many supplies, and even wages of personnel may be lower.

■ **More ability to negotiate.** When customers are harder to get, vendors are often more willing to do what it takes to close a deal. In addition to lower prices, you may be able to negotiate better payment or credit terms, free or low-cost add-ons, better service, and more.

■ **More available talent.** Typically, recessions also create higher unemployment—meaning it's easier for smaller and newer companies to attract high quality workers, often at lower salaries than in non-recessionary times. This creates an opportunity for you to build your team with top-notch people who are motivated to help you succeed.

In an economic downturn, a smart, nimble, hardworking competitor (that could be you!) often has a leg up, even on well-established big companies. You can go after their customers, devise new products or services to meet their changing needs, even look for weakened or disheartened competitors to acquire.

NOW WHAT?!

5. Take one step *TODAY*

Now, the most important thing you can do is to take action. We recommend doing at least one thing TODAY to make your business more resilient. In this book we've got 99 specific things you can do *right now* (or very soon) to survive and succeed.

So, as you read through this guide, seize on at least one tip you can do ASAP—preferably today. You'll find that taking action gives you back a bit that sense of taking control of your life as when you decided to start your own business.

And we know you've got it in you! Hey, if you wanted to play it safe, you'd still be at some old day job. But you wanted to take your life into your own hands, forge your own destiny. And you still do. You're an entrepreneur. The best thing you can do is take action. And take it soon.

Now's a good time to remind yourself why you went into business in the first place. Why did you want to own your own business? Be your own boss? Financial security? Time flexibility? Ability to use your skills? Keep those goals in mind. They're probably still motivating you.

- *Keep in mind:* if you have products or services people wanted and needed before the recession, they'll continue to want and need them.

- *Keep in mind:* you have it in you to forge your own destiny.

- *Keep in mind:* down economies present opportunities as well as challenges.

- *Keep in mind:* you'll have to work hard, make changes, face failures. But you have it in you to do all those things. As an entrepreneur, you knew there would be risk. You're not faint at heart.

Of course, you'll need to make some changes, but you can survive—you can even grow stronger and bigger. In a recession, one of your greatest strategic advantages may be your willingness to work hard, work smart, and keep at it, while others often are not.

Remember the excitement you felt when you first started your business? Try to recapture that sense of optimism, of taking charge of your future. Recommit to those goals, and, as you go through the tips in this book, consider at least one step you can take TODAY to get you closer to your goals.

FREE OR ON THE CHEAP

MEET WITH AN SBDC COUNSELOR. One of the best, least-known services provided by the U.S. Government to small businesses is a national network of Small Business Development Centers (SBDCs). There are over 1,000 SBDCs, located primarily at universities and community colleges.

Every year, SBDCs provide free one-on-one counseling and low-cost training programs to hundreds of thousands of small businesses and startup entrepreneurs. SBDC counselors are trained professionals; most have run small businesses and have management expertise. Since they've been around for over 35 years, you know the SBDCs have helped small businesses like yours weather past recessions—and they can help you with this one.

I highly recommend checking out your local SBDC sooner rather than later. You can find a link to a list of SBDCs online at https://americassbdc. org. Find your center and set up an appointment with a counselor to discuss your small business.

THE SH*T'S HIT THE FAN ...

NOW
WHAT?!

99 RECESSION-PROOF TIPS FOR
SMALL BUSINESS SUCCESS

START LEAN,
STAY LEAN

What you need to know since the sh*t's hit the fan.

The best way to survive and thrive is to be able to make changes to meet changing conditions. To do so, as we said in the last section, you have to be able to move quickly, try new things, see some of those new things fail, and make changes. That means being as light as you can—staying lean.

In a nutshell: staying "lean" means spending/buying/owning the least amount. This not only means you keep more of your money—it means you are less bogged down by the infrastructure and cost of your operations.

For example—a food truck is "leaner" than a brick-and-mortar restaurant. The owner of the food truck can literally move to find different customers, can easily change the type of food offered, has fewer employees, and has a vehicle lease instead of a long lease on a building. And a catering service might be even leaner than a food truck—if the owner used a commercial kitchen (rented facility) only when they had a gig. So—before you open a restaurant and take on all that "heavy" infrastructure, you can prove your concept, build your reputation, respond to changing conditions with a leaner approach to a cooked meal business.

In this step, we'll focus on how any business can start lean and stay lean.

NOW WHAT?!

6. Keep fixed costs down

When you run a business, you obviously have expenses. But not all expenses are alike.

First, you have "fixed" expenses that you have to pay every month—or week or year—regardless of how much you sell. Next, you have other expenses—"variable" expenses—that change depending on how much demand you have for your products or services. We'll deal with those in the very next tip.

Fixed expenses are expenses like rent, payment on term loans, equipment and vehicle leases, insurance, and any other expense you can't eliminate or reduce when sales drop.

Fixed expenses are often referred to as your overhead or "nut." Because you have so little flexibility with these expenses, they make it harder for you to be nimble, to pivot, to respond to changing conditions. These are the expenses that can actually cause you to shutter your business entirely. So, you need to do everything you can to reduce or eliminate fixed expenses to make your survival and success more likely.

What are some of the biggest fixed expenses you're likely to have and how can you deal with them?

Rent

This is the killer. For many small businesses dealing with the current economic situation and reduced sales, rent is the biggest expense that weighs on them month after month and can force them out of business. What can you do to reduce your rent?

■ **Renegotiate your lease.** If you already have space rented, now's the time for a conversation with your property manager or owner. Commercial real estate is facing a huge vacancy crisis as a result of the economic downturn. Most property owners can't afford to lose additional tenants. See if they will work with you to lower your monthly rent, delay payments, shorten the length of your lease, or otherwise help you stay in business. Of course, not all property managers are smart enough to work with small businesses, and that's such a mistake at this time.

■ **If you do have to enter into a lease, negotiate hard.** Try to make the lease as short as possible, have provisions allowing you to sublease, and—if at all possible—do not sign a lease where you have to give a personal guarantee (which means that if your business goes under, you are still personally responsible).

■ **Don't rent anything unless you have to.** If you're a startup or expanding into a new line of business, look for ways to do business without having ANY space of your own. Obviously, if you're a brick-and-mortar retailer or restaurant, that doesn't work. But if you are in other types of businesses—services, technology, construction—see if you can find other spaces to work at/from, whether work-from-home, work-from-truck, or other locations you might be able to use.

■ **Use "rent-as-you-go" space.** In the last few years, a number of temporary work spaces have popped up—not just shared work spaces with desks for techies, but rental kitchens (for catering companies, meal delivery services, food product companies) and other short-term, rent-by-the-day or hour types of spaces. Some of these have closed temporarily or permanently due to Covid-19 impact, but search them out in your area. If necessary, reach out to local businesses that are likely to have extra space to see if you can rent that space on an "as needed" basis. One other source to check out is LiquidSpace—www.liquidspace. com—a site that lists spaces you can rent hourly or monthly.

Term loans and equipment/vehicle leases

Now is also the time to reexamine, renegotiate, and look for alternatives to any and all of your long-term financial obligations, especially those that charge interest.

Interest rates are, at the time of this writing, at a very low rate. So, the first thing to do is to negotiate with your vendor. Perhaps they would be willing to lower your interest rate—and thus, your monthly payment. Perhaps they would be willing to allow you to forgo a number of current payments—tacking them on to the end of the term—to help you weather the current situation.

Another option is to look for other sources with lower interest rates or more forgiving payment options—such as a new loan, line-of-credit, or SBA/other government financing program—that would enable you to pay off this fixed expense now and replace it with a lower cost option.

Expenses that look fixed but really aren't

Many of your monthly bills come regularly and are always the same amount. But there's probably some room for you to lower those costs. For instance, you probably use a number of cloud-based services—you may be able to reduce the level of service or number of seats you are paying for. Or you have insurance that provides a certain level of coverage or add-on coverages. You may be able to reduce those amounts.

Negotiate everything! Just because it's a recurring monthly bill, don't imagine there's no room for negotiation—even with the largest corporations. Perhaps you chose a company because of a tempting "introductory offer" three years ago, but that $39 a month is probably $150 a month now. Here's a dirty little secret: Companies know you get busy, and they slowly raise prices, especially on long-term customers. I'm betting your insurance—whether it's health, liability, vehicle, or fire—has increased substantially since you chose your provider.

So schedule a morning SOON to examine each and every bill you have and see how you can lower those costs or eliminate them altogether.

7. Reduce variable expenses

Variable expenses—inventory, raw materials, staff—sound easy to reduce, since they change depending on how much demand there is for your products or services. You need less stuff when you have fewer sales, right?

Not so fast. It's not—usually—an immediate relationship between a customer or client wanting your products or services and you providing them. You need inventory to be able to entice and sell to your customers. You need staff, and often space, to be able to provide your services. You need raw materials to manufacture your products. That means making decisions about purchasing before you actually make a sale.

To reduce your variable expenses, there are a number of strategies—including some in the tips that follow this one. But in general, when dealing with variable expenses, to give you the most leeway and buy you the most time, keep the following in mind:

■ **Choose vendors based on more than competitive prices.** Look for their ability to fill orders fast, give you more generous payment terms (such as more time to pay your bills), their reliability, and the ability for you to pay with credit cards if you need to.

■ **Purchase carefully.** Examine past sales records, do your research and forecast sales conservatively, especially in this environment. It may be better to lose a sale than to spend too much on inventory, raw materials, or supplies.

Be certain to look at all recurring expenses—any bill you pay at least once a year and especially once a month—and negotiate.

Here's how:

■ **Collect your paperwork.** Gather the most recent statements of ALL accounts you pay regularly, not just monthly, but quarterly, semiannually, and annually. Remember to check your credit card statements for accounts that bill automatically, such as online services or web hosting.

■ **Do research.** Look up prices, advertisements, and promotions for all the services you use, both from your vendors and their competitors. Through social media, ask other business owners which services they're using and if they'll tell you how much they are paying. These give you ammunition when negotiating.

■ **Make the call.** Set aside a few hours, preferably in the morning, to make phone calls. For each account, call your sales representative, agent, or the customer service number, and do the following:

■ **Ask to lower your rate.** Yes, this seems daunting, but it's surprisingly uncomplicated. Just say, "Hi, I see I'm paying a rate of 'X.' You're offering a lower rate to new customers; I'd like that rate applied to me." Or, "I'm considering switching suppliers, (cancelling my service, credit card, whatever), unless you can offer me a substantially lower rate. What can we work out?"

■ **Negotiate.** Don't take a simple "No" or "That's our standard rate" for an answer. Ask to speak to someone who has authority to discount your rates. Most companies will offer you something, especially if you're a good customer. Mention the other prices or deals you've seen or been offered by other companies.

■ **Be willing to switch.** You may get a much better deal from a different company, and it helps your negotiating stance if you're truly willing to leave your current provider. If changing providers is not very disruptive to your company and you save a lot of money, be ready to make that step.

■ **Be courteous.** The goal is to have vendors want to keep you as a customer. If you're belligerent, they'll be happy to see you go.

■ **Ask for good customer discounts.** Most companies—especially shipping companies—have discounts for larger customers. Ask them to provide you with those rates, even though you are a small business, if only for a year. Appeal to their sense of civic pride that they are helping a small business survive in a time of crisis.

NOW WHAT?!

8. Embrace MVP

If you've been in business for some time, you're almost certainly proud of the quality and completeness of the products or services you offer. Indeed, for many small businesses, "quality" is their competitive advantage.

That's why it may be hard to understand the approach you now need to take when you are "pivoting"—changing business directions to respond to changing conditions, introducing new products or services to meet changing customer needs.

As you innovate—as you think like a startup—you need to embrace the concept of "MVP," or minimal viable product.

Basically, a minimal viable product is a product or service that has been created quickly, meeting only the absolutely necessary level of quality to meet customers' basic needs, in order to get it to market as soon as possible. Over time, and seeing the experience of actual customers, the product is improved and refined and revised.

Google's product development mantra, for instance, is "Experiment, expedite, iterate." In other words, the company tries a lot of new things, moves quickly rather than getting stuck, and refines and improves along the way.

Clearly you don't want a minimally viable product for a medical device or automobile where health and safety is of great concern. But for most products and services—especially in today's climate—consumers are willing, even eager, to get the Version 1.0 of a new product or service that better meets their current needs. So keep MVP in mind as you experiment with new products and services—and you can become an MVP yourself.

NOW WHAT?!

9. Fail fast

In this environment, you're going to have to try many new things to survive and succeed. Some of them will work—and you'll come out ahead. But some of them will flop, and you need to be prepared for some failure.

Great entrepreneurs are good at failing. I often tell budding entrepreneurs the key to success is to be able to take failure and learn from it. You have to treat each failure as a momentary experience, not let it define and deter you. But that's only possible if you're willing to critically learn from why you failed, keep the costs of your failures limited, and move on—better able to succeed.

To succeed, you have to learn the right way to fail:

- **Fail Fast.** Try new things without obsessing about perfection. Develop things quickly, then get them out the door—that's embracing the MVP approach. You need real world feedback from customers, users, partners to be able to fix your mistakes. To fail fast, give employees authority to make decisions, act on them without a lot of hassle. If things don't work out, move on quickly, without a lot of self-recrimination or criticism of others.

- **Fail forward.** Fail in a way that moves your company, products, services in a new direction. It is certainly possible to fail backward—doing things you've done before, trying to recapture past glories, or what made you a success a decade ago. Failure only leads to success if you're stretching yourself, trying new things, innovating. Move fast and move forward.

- **Fail smart.** You don't learn much, or gain much, if you fail because you're doing something clearly avoidable. Take care of business fundamentals, pay your bills, motivate your employees, communicate. Failure is only useful if you're learning something from it.

- **Fail cheap.** Try to keep your financial losses from a failure as minimal as possible. One way to do this is to start new things "lean"—with the least amount of investment to test the concept. Remember, it doesn't have to be—shouldn't be—perfect.

NOW WHAT?!

10. Reduce inventory

Never forget this phrase: "Inventory is money sitting around in a different form." Remember that concept every time you look at the stuff you sell. You've already paid for those jeans hanging from racks in your clothing store, the snowboards you have in your ski shop, the raw materials you have in your manufacturing plant. You've already paid the vendor (or put it on your credit card) for the boxes of blank T-shirts you hope to screen print as soon as you get orders.

You can't put the money that's tied up in inventory—whether raw materials or finished products—to work for you. You can't spend that money on experimenting with new business lines, marketing or hiring a new salesperson, or paying your rent or health insurance. And you can't use it to pay down your line-of-credit or credit cards. After all, credit card companies don't accept T-shirts as a form of payment.

If you're just starting in business—or trying new things in your existing business—you want to build in practices that keep your inventory levels always as low as possible. But if you're already in business with inventory sitting around, what can you do to turn that inventory into ready cash? What are some effective ways for you to move your products or services?

- **Multiple purchase or bulk purchase discounts.** Whether it's a "two for one," "buy one, get one free," or steep discounts for bulk purchases, motivate customers to buy more than one product or service at a time.

- **Bundles.** "Package" a number of products or services into one "product" with a large overall discount. This gives the buyer a very high perceived value and moves a lot of merchandise at once.

- **Specials.** Identify your excess inventory as your "Special of the Day" or week. Customers are attracted to specials. Many restaurants know this technique—their specials of the day are often the food they had the most left over from the previous days.

■ **Extremely steep discounts.** These have to be significant (40–50% or more) but of a limited time only so you don't train customers to expect those discounts—to motivate customers to buy NOW.

■ **Gifts to referral sources.** Use your products or services as an incentive to get others to become salespeople for you. "Get one free with each new customer you refer."

■ **Gifts to good customers.** Use products or services that you know customers aren't going to buy as a retention and mechanism for building good will.

■ **Donate for marketing purposes.** As a final resort, give your products or services to organizations that can raise your visibility, such as local public radio stations, community events, schools.

NOW WHAT?!

11. Learn to love "just-in-time"

How much money you've got tied up in inventory, raw materials, or finished product sitting in your warehouse, your retail store, or your backroom makes a direct impact on your bottom line. It's not just simply taking up space; it's money sitting around, losing value.

Of course, if you don't have sufficient inventory, you occasionally can't make sales. Every business dreads the possibility of receiving lucrative orders it can't fill due to inadequate supplies. And sometimes you don't only lose sales; you lose a customer. This is the risk in maintaining too low an inventory.

The answer is to develop inventory management systems that get you the stuff you need just when you need it. The business term for that is "just-in-time." The goal is to reduce the amount of stuff you have to pay for before your customers pay you. Ideally, you pay your suppliers no earlier (and perhaps later) than your customers pay you.

While just-in-time is a concept that came about in manufacturing, it's equally applicable in retail, hospitality, and many service businesses.

Imagine, for example, if you ran a restaurant, and your kitchen only received the raw food from your supplier once a customer placed their order—and voila!—you were able to serve the diner hot food in time without owning any food in your refrigerators. That would certainly make a restaurant more profitable, as it wouldn't have any wasted food (that the restaurant, of course, had to pay for).

Or consider, for example, if you ran a hair salon and the color you needed for a specific customer only showed up when the customer made an appointment—eliminating your need for the inventory of a whole stock of hair color. That would save you money.

We can't do those things quite yet, but just-in-time is developing in many industries, and given today's needs for all businesses to run leaner, I suspect we'll see some innovations in many other industries. In book publishing, for example, print on demand (POD) has been rapidly growing. As a result of very fast, efficient book-printing machines, a "one-off" book can be printed quickly just when a customer orders the book and then shipped to the customer. That is already being done for books that are out of print or not in great demand. POD printing is still considerably more expensive in relationship to big printing presses for popular books that can be printed in bulk, but the costs are shrinking, and that is the wave of the future for that industry.

Of course, just-in-time has its downsides, including:

■ **Paying more per item.** Because you are not placing large orders, and because it is often considerably more expensive for a vendor to fulfill last-minute orders, costs are higher.

■ **Potential for supplies not to arrive in time.** Because you have reduced the time between ordering and the time you need to actually use a product, there's more room for errors, shipping lags, and slipups to occur.

■ **Potential to lose quality.** Since just-in-time might mean rush orders on the part of your supplier, quality may be somewhat reduced.

To improve your ability to reduce your inventory and move to a more just-in-time like ordering process, do the following:

■ **Seek out vendors with the fastest turn-around times.** That means you can order closer to when you actually need to use a product—and you can make changes in your purchasing patterns based on more real-time demands.

■ **Seek out local vendors.** If a vendor is closer to you—geographically—it means faster shipping times (and typically, lower shipping costs).

■ **Be your vendors' favorite customer.** No, as a small business you can't be their biggest customer—but you can be one of their favorites. That means paying on time, communicating clearly and often, being appreciative, getting to know them and having them get to know you. This will pay off big time if you have a situation where you need something fast. They'll be more willing to go the extra mile for someone they like.

■ **Improve the flow of information from sales teams to purchasing teams.** In a small business, that may just mean checking in daily with your front-line sales people to see what is selling and what is not, or having detailed point-of-sales systems that give you detailed insight into your sales. This doesn't necessarily have to be technologically advanced. Decades ago, See's Candy had someone from each of its retail stores daily telephone in sales figures on each type of candy to headquarters so the company could see which candies it needed to make the next day.

■ **Get customers to pre-order.** The longer in advance that you know what a customer wants, the more time you have to get the materials, inventory, or supplies you need. Providing a discount to customers as an incentive for pre-orders, especially pre-paid orders, helps you significantly reduce the inventory you need on hand and may more than offset the lower price you charge.

FREE OR ON THE CHEAP

INVENTORY MANAGEMENT SOFTWARE. Several companies offer free bare-bones versions of their inventory management software systems. A few to check out:

■ **Odoo** (www.odoo.com)

■ **inFlow Inventory** (www.inflowinventory.com)

■ **Sortly** (www.sortly.com)

---

12. Have your vendors "own" your inventory

The absolute best just-in-time inventory is one in which you never actually own anything you sell until you actually sell it. Ideally, you wouldn't ever touch the product or service you sell.

Jeff Bezos started the "largest bookstore in the world" without ever owning a book. In fact, he didn't even have to ship the book a customer ordered. Instead, he was smart enough to identify that the bookselling industry had distributors and wholesalers who stocked huge inventories of books, which they could send to customers directly when Amazon placed an order. In that way, Bezos was able to spend his money on building his online "bookstore" without having to spend his funds on actual books.

You've now probably seen thousands of online "stores" that are doing exactly what Bezos did at first. They create an attractive "storefront"—in this case, a website—that advertises and merchandises products (or others' services) and then forwards that order onto a distributor, wholesaler, or other vendor who has the inventory, fulfills the order in the name of the storefront, and in some cases, even uses packaging with the name of the reseller.

The name for this kind of arrangement is "dropshipping," and it's a very attractive arrangement. You can start selling a type of product with virtually no upfront cost or commitment. You can offer many more products, and you don't tie up your money in inventory.

This is different than being an "affiliate" of another retailer. In this kind of arrangement, you still "own" the customer. You market to and find the customer, you bill the customer, you provide customer support, and you would be stuck with any non-payment. As a result, you earn far more on each sale than you would as just an affiliate or conduit bringing customers to some other business.

Of course, you don't make as much money on each sale doing this as you would if you actually maintained the inventory yourself. The vendor either gives you a smaller discount since they are taking on the risk of inventory and the cost of fulfillment and/or they charge you extra fees. But you have far less financial risk.

You don't have to do this only with a web storefront. Whatever line of business you are in, investigate if there are suppliers who will quickly fulfill orders for you when you have an order.

Seek out distributors and wholesalers who will do direct fulfillment of their inventory for you and bill you as products are shipped. If you run an ecommerce on Shopify, they have a service called Oberlo, www.Oberlo. com, to help you find dropship goods and suppliers.

13. Cut waste

Whenever you see waste, you're looking at something you paid for and didn't consume. It might be excess inventory, excessive raw materials, excess packaging on your products, delivery packaging, even lights and heat left on when no one is present. All those things add up to money—your money—going to waste.

In the "Operations" section, we'll give you more specific tips on how to cut waste. But if you want to start lean and stay lean, you have to become single-mindedly determined to cut waste. Make sure everyone who works with you—whether staff, subcontractors, delivery personnel—understands just how much you hate waste. Examine every aspect of your business to be more efficient, use fewer resources, and cut out waste. Waste, of any kind, wastes your money.

STAY SANE!

Don't be hard on yourself

In this unprecedented economic environment, things won't be up to your usual standards so give yourself a break. You might create a minimal viable product that flops. Or you pivot so quickly that you slap up a website literally overnight that you ordinarily would spend weeks on. Perhaps you simply can't work the hours you once did, due to stress, anxiety, and all kinds of distractions. Right now, the world is going to be hard enough on you; you don't have to be hard on yourself.

THE SH*T'S HIT THE FAN ...

NOW
WHAT?!

99 RECESSION-PROOF TIPS FOR
SMALL BUSINESS SUCCESS

MAKE THE
MOST OF YOUR
MONEY

What you need to know since the sh*t's hit the fan.

Virtually every small business owners worries about money. But in this economic environment, with such an uncertain future, managing money is even more critical now for your small business survival. Every dollar counts. And you need to count every dollar.

First, a couple of basic things to remember:

■ **Cash is king.** If the three most significant things in real estate are "location, location, location," the three most important things in business are "cash, cash, cash." In normal times, a smart business also looks at 'profitability'—which product or service lines have the best return on investment. You don't have time for that right now. Instead, concentrate on making sales and getting cash, even if it means you have small profit margins. Money in the bank is going to enable you to survive until times get better (and they will).

■ **Credit is queen.** Most small businesses rightfully hate being in debt. But having good credit—and using it wisely—is an important tool in your management toolbox, especially now. Don't get overloaded on debt, but don't be afraid of it either. (See the next section "Be Smart About Financing" on how to get and use credit wisely.)

14. Spend money wisely

While you need to watch your spending, don't be so obsessed with lowering expenses that you cut things that bring you money or help you survive, such as:

■ **Staying in front of your current customers and prospects.** You should regularly be sending out email newsletters, posting and boosting on social media, making calls. Let your current and past customers know how they can buy from you now. Offer discounts, weekly specials, sell gift cards, provide delivery. Do what it takes to get them to open their wallets.

■ **Safety and cleanliness.** In this pandemic-impacted world, if you have a place of business, whether a retail store, a restaurant, a factory, an office: cleanliness is now job one. Customers and employees will not return if they feel they are not safe. If any kind of outbreak happens at your place of business, you'll be set back even further than you are now. Spend money on having employees continually disinfect, providing hand sanitizer and face masks. Require masks on customers for in-person interactions. It is unfair to your employees to force them to interact with customers not wearing masks.

■ **Pivoting.** You are almost certainly going to have to make some changes in your business to meet the new realities. That's going to cost some money—whether it's implementing new technology, changing facilities, engaging new employees or consultants to help you execute on those changes. Spend money necessary to change your business practices to meet the needs of this new world.

NOW
WHAT?!

15. Get help

Before we go much farther into the world of money management, here's an important thing to remember—you don't have to be a whiz with numbers or a financial genius to run a successful business. You don't have to do these things yourself, but you do need to know how to get help with your finances, accounting, billing, money management if you're not good at it yourself.

It is far better to hire someone to send out invoices for you once a month, or even once a week, than not to send out your invoices 'til six months after you've done the work or delivered the goods. It's better to hire someone to help you pay your bills than to let your bills go unpaid and incur hefty late fees, interest, and penalties.

Having a really good accountant who can help you figure out how to save money on taxes—and ensures you pay them on time—can save you thousands of dollars, and perhaps even save your business.

If you need financial help, get it.

NOW WHAT?!

16. Get a business bank account

Many self-employed and very small businesses just use personal bank accounts to manage their business bills and income. After all, it may cost you a small amount of money each month to have a business account with a bank or credit union.

But one thing we learned during the initial Covid-19 shut-down and PPP (Payroll Protection Plan) program was that those companies that had pre-existing **business** relationships with a bank or credit union were in a far better position for getting government help. In fact, some banks would not work with anyone who did NOT have a business banking relationship, regardless of how much money they had in personal accounts.

If you do not already have a business bank account for your business, now's the time to get one. And consider looking at community banks and credit unions, not just big national banks, where you can get to know your banker, and your banker can get to know you.

17. Set up your books

In this economic environment, it's critical to keep a close eye on your company's finances. You can't do that if you don't have a good bookkeeping program or app. Having decent bookkeeping is particularly important now, when your business may qualify for government assistance or you need to get a loan. You'll need decent financial records to apply for and qualify for that kind of financial help. And if you're unfortunate enough to find yourself facing a disaster, such as hurricane, fire, flood, good financial records will make it far faster and easier to apply for and receive government disaster aid or insurance.

The tried-and-true leader in small business accounting programs is Quickbooks by Intuit (www.quickbooks.intuit.com). They have a variety of different options depending on the nature and size of your business. Their online app—QBO or Quickbooks Online—is simple to use and not very expensive. But there are plenty of other options, including Xero (www.xero.com), Freshbooks (www.freshbooks.com), and Zoho Books (www.zoho.com/us/books).

FREE OR ON THE CHEAP

MONEY MANAGEMENT APPS. In addition to paid versions, the following apps have free plans with enough features for some small businesses to get started with:

- ■ **Harvest** (www.getharvest.com)

- ■ **Wave** (www.waveapps.com)

- ■ **Mint** (www.mint.com)

- ■ **Everlance** (www.everlance.com)

---

18. Watch your cash flow like a hawk

As we said at the beginning of this section—and something you should never forget—cash is king. Right now, the most important financial aspect of your business is having enough cash on hand to pay your bills. Every dollar that you have in the bank means that much longer you can stay in business. And the longer you can stay in business, the longer you'll have for the economy to recover, and you can start making bigger profits.

Since managing your cash is key to business survival, your "Cash Flow Statement" will be your most important financial assessment for monitoring how much money you receive and how much you spend. Your "Income Statement" or "Profit or Loss" statement lets you know if you are making a profit, and that's important, of course. In non-recessionary times, that may be equally important as cash flow. But you can be making a profit and not have enough money to pay your bills. And if you can't pay your employees, your bills, or yourself, you won't stay in business long. Even profitable firms can—and do—go out of business due to cash flow problems.

In recessionary times, it's even harder to generate positive cash flow because your customers may pay late, especially if yours is a business where you bill clients rather than collect immediately. Surprisingly, this may be equally true whether your clients are large corporations, small businesses, or consumers.

So in these times, you need to start paying closer attention to your cash flow: when are your "accounts receivable"—outstanding invoices—realistically likely to be paid, and when are your "accounts payable"—your bills—due.

Your bookkeeping app or software should be able to generate your Cash Flow statement (especially if you are entering invoices and bills regularly—which is a good habit to get into) and PlanningShop's pre-formatted, Excel-based Business Plan Financials make the process of creating your financial statements, like cash flow, easier and faster, especially for startups and new business lines. Purchase and download instantly at www. planningshop.com.

19. Get paid faster

Since every dollar counts right now, make it as easy as possible for customers to pay you as fast as possible. There are many ways to do this so that your customers see it as a benefit rather than a negative. One way, of course, is to accept credit cards—see the next tip. But there are a few other techniques.

- **Eliminate or reduce billing.** If you typically bill your clients for goods or services, it often takes at least 30-60 days for you to get paid. Occasionally you don't get paid at all. That's tough on your cash flow and your profitability. Instead, require, or at least request, payment on delivery or pre-payment. Even if you are a professional service provider—like a lawyer, accountant, dentist, doctor, consultant—you can require payment at the time the service is given, or even require an upfront payment at the time the appointment is made. If you worry that this seems unprofessional, realize that this is a changed world, and clients are becoming more used to paying as they go for such services. Eliminating billing means you'll have your money faster and have less paperwork too.

- **Offer incentives for early payment.** If you are hesitant to demand pre-payment or payment on delivery, consider giving customers a small discount for paying early, such as paying within 10 days of receipt of invoice. Yes, this will cost you a bit, but you'll get your money immediately and improve your cash flow.

- **Offer gift cards.** While these are called "gift cards," they are really "pre-payment" cards. Gift cards are a way for customers to pay long before anyone receives your product or service. That means more money in your bank account. And while they are called "cards," they may actually be digital credits connected to your point-of-sale or credit card processing software. There's more on gift cards in the section "Make Sales."

20. Accept credit cards

One tried-and-true way to get paid faster is to accept credit cards as a form of payment.

Surprisingly, many small businesses do not accept credit cards. Traditionally, professional services sent out invoices and got paid by check. Many small retailers, contractors, and service businesses don't want to pay the processing fees and only accept cash.

But when you accept credit cards, you enable customers to pay you immediately and you get the money in your bank fast—often the day after processing. Yes, you pay a transaction fee for this benefit, but you don't have to worry about checks bouncing or invoices not getting paid.

You may also enable more customers to buy from you. Many customers no longer carry cash, or they want to only do business with "cashless" and "touchless" businesses. And some customers are committed to the credit cards—wanting to earn points for miles and purchases.

Of course, you need to weigh the costs of accepting credit cards, especially if you have a client with a very large bill. It's heart-stopping to have to pay the transaction fee—which can be upwards of 3%—on a $10,000 invoice. But if you have any inkling that that customer may not pay, or pay very late, you're far, far better paying the transaction fee than losing the income altogether.

One way to accept credit cards easily: **Get a mobile credit card reader with POS (Point Of Sale) system.** If you don't already accept credit cards, or if you make sales to customers when you're away from your place of business, you can get a credit card merchant account that has pre-determined, fairly reasonable processing fees. Many of these come with both mobile credit card readers that attach to your mobile phone or tablet and systems you can use at your place of business, particularly at check-out counters. A few of the best known of these include:

- **Square** (www.squareup.com)
- **QuickBooks GoPayment** (www.gopayment.com)
- **PayPal Here** (www.paypalhere.com)

21. Send out your invoices quickly

If in fact there is no way to avoid sending invoices to customers or clients, the key to getting paid faster is to get those invoices out quickly. Many small business owners, especially consultants and professionals, often wait for two, three, even more months before sending a bill. That's a guaranteed way to damage your cash flow. You need every dollar you can get NOW, so get those invoices out NOW.

So, first, if you have any work or products you've already delivered that you have not billed for—send those invoices out TODAY. That's right—today. Carve out time today to send out invoices for any work you've already done or goods you've provided that you haven't billed for. Don't wait a day more.

In the future, regularly set aside a time—at least once a month but preferably once a week or as soon as you complete the work or deliver the goods— to prepare and send out your invoices. Get them out and then follow up if clients are late in paying. You deserve to get paid for the work you have already performed. And you need that money in your bank account.

If you really can't do this yourself—you either don't seem to have the time, capability, or inclination to send out your invoices regularly—GET HELP. Hire someone to meet with you once a week, twice a month, or at least once a month—to go over your billings and send out those invoices!

22. Defer payments

There are two ways to keep more money in your bank account: get paid faster and pay others slower. While doing everything you can to get cash in your bank account sooner, find ways to delay depleting that stash for as long as possible. Of course, these ways should:

1. Be legal

2. Not be costly (in terms of fees, interest)

3. Maintain good relationship with your vendors

4. Help other small businesses survive

5. Not keep you up at night

Fortunately, there are a number of ways you can do this.

- **Ask for installment payments.** For large bills, ask vendors if you can pay in installments over three to six months, without incurring any interest payments. While these types of arrangements might be unusual in normal times, right now vendors are more likely to be willing to work with you. BUT—be sure to make every payment on time. If need be, have interest accrue only if you pay each installment late.

- **Negotiate payment terms.** Ask your vendor to extend the amount of time you have to pay your bills, ideally to Net 60 or Net 90. If you ask BEFORE you make the purchase, you'll have more negotiating leverage. If you have an existing relationship with a vendor—and a stellar payment record—you can certainly ask for such terms now.

- **Pay by credit card.** This automatically provides you with longer payment terms—approximately 30 extra days. That means you keep more money in your bank account for about a month. You might also get credit card "points" that you can use—not just for airline miles but to make necessary purchases. Of course, you must have the discipline (and the money) to pay your card off on time; otherwise you'll be paying hefty interest charges. Look for vendors who accept credit card payments.

■ **Use your line of credit.** If you have set up a line of credit with your bank or credit union (see the section on financing), you can use the funds available on your line. You will pay interest fees on these expenses the minute you use them. However, if your vendor doesn't accept credit cards and/or you know you will not be able to pay off the amount before your credit card bill would be due, the interest rate on credit lines tend to be far, far lower than credit card interest rates.

■ **Use a third-party credit card acceptance provider.** This is an expensive solution, but if you really need to put something on a credit card and your vendor does not accept credit cards and you're stuck, you can use a third party company that accepts your credit card, pays the bill, and charges you a fee. One such company is Plastiq (www.plastiq.com) which at the time of this writing charged 2.5% of the bill ON TOP of whatever you pay to the vendor and the credit card company.

STAY SANE!

Watch out for scams

During a crisis, scammers prey on small business owners who would otherwise pay closer attention during normal times. Fake invoices, fake orders, and fake threats to shut off your utilities unless you hand over your credit card information are just a few of the most common cons scammers will target small businesses with. For more guidance on scams to watch out for, go to the Federal Trade Commission's website (www.ftc.gov/tips-advice/business-center/guidance/scams-your-small-business-guide-business).

THE SH*T'S HIT THE FAN ...

NOW
WHAT?!

99 RECESSION-PROOF TIPS FOR
SMALL BUSINESS SUCCESS

BE SMART
ABOUT
FINANCING

What you need to know since the sh*t's hit the fan.

Right now, with the business world so uncertain, every small business owner needs every dollar they can get their hands on. Even if you don't currently feel you need money, you want to be in a good position to get the money when you do need it.

Given the uncertainty of the economy, it may be easier to get financial help now than it will be later, when banks and credit cards may tighten up their lending criteria. And if your business isn't in trouble, it's a good idea to take advantage of any financing opportunities you have now as you may be more credit-worthy now than later. Who knows what tomorrow may bring?

You may tempted to take any money you can find. Exercise care first. The various sources of money cost you very different amounts—whether in terms of interest rates, fees, or the returns investors are looking for on their investments. So be savvy about financing options.

And, of course, be careful. In this section, I'm going to tell you how to get more credit available to you. But that doesn't mean you should go out and run up a bunch of debt.

Credit and debt are tools for your business: you have to use them carefully and only as and when needed. You don't want to get into more debt than you can realistically pay back—or in so much debt that you can't sleep at night.

23. Get the best money of all

Before we talk about ways to get financing, never forget that the very best money of all comes from actually making sales of your product or service to customers. Now you may think that making more sales is out of your reach, especially in this economic climate, but I want you to seriously consider sales as your first financing choice.

Think of the benefits: You neither have to give up a piece of your company (as with investors) nor do you take on debt (as with a loan). When you need money to stay afloat, pivot, start, or maybe grow—look seriously at whether there are ways for you to find money through sales.

Now, if you're an existing business, your sales may be down dramatically, so the idea of finding money through sales is daunting. And if you're just launching certain types of businesses, such as retail stores, restaurants, and new manufacturing businesses, you'll typically need significant financing up front before you can make your first sale.

Remember, consider this a "spaghetti year"—you may have to throw a lot of different things at the wall to see what sticks. Figure out how you can use what you already have—or can acquire cheaply—to generate new types of sales. Keep costs down and think of low-cost "prototypes" to help you determine where you can generate sales before you invest a lot.

So before you go look for investors or take on debt, see the "Make Sales" section to get ideas on how you can improve your sales and get money coming in.

24. Check your credit reports

When you own a small business or are self-employed, your personal credit and your business credit are entwined. Typically, you're going to have to give a personal guarantee for any business loan, to sign a lease, buy a van, or get credit terms from your vendors. Business creditors are going to check your personal credit score. So pay attention!

You'll want to get your credit reports—not just your credit score—so you can correct any errors or mistakes and better understand what is affecting your credit score. Many credit card companies may allow you to quickly check your credit score. While your credit score is useful to know—and will affect the interest you pay on credit—you need your full credit REPORTS to see if there are any errors. Check the reports from the three major credit reporting agencies: Equifax, Experian, and TransUnion.

Once a year, by law, you're entitled to a free credit report from all three major credit reporting agencies. During the Covid-19 crisis, they're providing free online reports weekly through April, 2021. Here's the link where you go to get your official free credit report: www.AnnualCreditReport.com.

Beware! There are other sites that purport to offer you free credit reports, but this is the one and only official site for your free credit reports as mandated by the government. The others are likely to charge you.

25. Clean up your credit

Once you have your hands on your full credit reports, review them carefully. Take steps to challenge or clean up any mistaken information. Even small mistakes can cost you in higher interest rates or cause you to be turned down for credit. Years ago, the bad credit of another "Rhonda Abrams"— with a completely different social security number and address—ended up on my credit report. It took a while to get that off my record, so check your credit reports soon!

Go over each of your credit reports thoroughly, checking to see if there is ANYTHING inaccurate. Be certain to search for any debts that are not yours. Look at any "dings" on your report—late payments, failure to pay, and so on—and make certain those are all accurate. If anything is wrong, contact the credit bureau and dispute the report. If you have past-due accounts, you can contact the company that gave you credit to see if they'll ask the credit agency to remove the report. You're more likely to be successful at that if the bill is old, if you've been a good customer since you last had the problem, and if they just are willing to work with you.

Put any unresolved dispute in writing and send it to the credit bureau, asking that your comments be added to your file. That may not change your credit score, but it won't hurt to have the information in there.

Be sure to check all your personal details. If any information on your report doesn't belong to you, it may be a sign of either identity theft or that someone else's credit is also being merged with yours.

NOW WHAT?!

26. Get—or increase—a line of credit

The most traditional form of business credit is an LOC—or "line of credit" (sometimes referred to as a "line")—from a bank or credit union. If you have a good relationship with a bank or credit union, you definitely want to explore setting up a credit line or increasing the amount on your line, especially in these uncertain times.

A credit line is a "revolving" borrowing capability. The financial institution sets a certain maximum amount that you can call upon to borrow when you need it. You can borrow some or all of that amount. It gives you flexibility and quick access to funds when you encounter a short-term cash crunch. A credit line is designed to meet short-term cash flow needs—not long-term debt—so typically you must "zero out" or pay off the loan amount at least once each year.

You can use a credit line much like you use a credit card—buying something, paying some bills when you're short of cash for a month or a few months, and then paying off the balance. The interest rate for a line of credit, fortunately, is far lower than on a credit card. Typically, it's a few points above "prime rate"—based on the rate the Federal government charges financial institutions for borrowing money—making it a fairly reasonable rate. You may also pay an annual fee for the line of credit.

A credit line usually is not secured by any collateral, but as the business owner, you'll almost certainly have to sign a personal guaranty for this loan, just as for any other business loan.

Remember—however—that having a credit line doesn't mean you HAVE to use it. It's just another option for you to increase your borrowing capability during a difficult economic period. Talk to your business banker to set up an LOC or increase the amount available if you already have a line of credit, so you'll have credit available if you need.

27. Increase credit limits on your credit cards

You've probably got a number of credit cards you can use to help finance bills for your business. When you first got each card, the issuer set a credit limit—or the maximum amount you could charge. That number may never have changed since you first got the credit card.

If you've been a smart user of credit, your credit card issuer may be willing to increase the amount you can borrow—increase your credit limit. Now—when you may need access to more credit—is the time to see if you can get those credit lines increased.

How do you do it? Simple. You pick up the phone. Call the number on the back of the card or on your bill and ask. You may have to talk to a couple of different people, answer some questions, perhaps fill out a form. But it's worth trying.

Of course, if you are already overextended—both on the specific card you're calling about or on your overall credit—you're not likely to get your credit lines increased.

Once again, just because you have more credit available doesn't mean you should rush to use it. It's just an insurance policy to have in case you need it. Don't just spend it because you have it—or have access to it. Remember, part of your credit score is how much credit you have available to you versus how much you are using.

Always use credit cards carefully. Credit cards are one of the most expensive ways to carry debt. So try to use credit cards only for debts you can pay off within the month as much as possible.

NOW WHAT?!

28. Get government help

In normal times, there is limited financial help available from the US Government for small businesses. The best-known programs are the SBA (Small Business Administration) guaranteed loan (7a program) to cover operating expenses or the SBA 504 program to acquire fixed assets such as buildings or large equipment. These loans are administered by banks and other lending institutions. You need to provide a personal guarantee and must demonstrate the capability of repaying the loan.

After emergencies—floods, earthquakes, hurricanes, fires, and the like— the SBA often steps in with their emergency loan programs, such as the Economic Injury Disaster Loan (EIDL). These are extremely helpful to businesses that have been hit by such emergencies.

During the national Covid-19 emergency, the US government enacted a few special programs to provide greater help to a greater range of small businesses. Some of these programs did not require a personal guaranty— making them more attractive as the business owner did not have to put their home or savings at risk. They also had more generous terms, both in interest rates and how long a company had to repay the loan. A couple of these programs were the PPP—Paycheck Protection Program and an expanded EIDL program.

It's worthwhile to stay informed as to what programs the government— and state and local agencies—may enact or extend to help small businesses with financing. In addition to following the news and any information from your community or industry, contact your local Small Business Development Center (www.americassbdc.org) for any information they may have on government financial help.

29. Consider investors

Realistically, at any time, it's tough for a small business or a startup to raise money from investors. Sure, you've heard all those stories of Silicon Valley twenty-somethings raising millions for their app, but those are the rare exceptions, not the rule. Yes, perhaps your rich aunt would "invest" in your startup or your father-in-law would help bail out your struggling business. But raising money has always been tough.

Challenging economic times make finding investors even tougher. But that doesn't mean that it never happens. The key is to find an investor who understands your story and believes in you.

One source might be a "strategic" investor—someone with a related business that knows your strengths and believes that an investment in your company will pay off in the long run. This person might be in your industry or in your community.

The other option is a traditional one: "friends and family." These are people who want to see you succeed—or at least not to fail—and they're willing to open their wallets to help you out.

30. Check out crowdfunding

sOne additional source of potential funds can actually come from strangers—that is if you have a compelling idea or you have a large group of committed customers who want to help you through this difficult time.

Through online crowdfunding platforms—such as Kickstarter (www.kickstarter.com) or IndieGoGo (www.indiegogo.com)—and with a concerted campaign to drive support through social media and other channels, you may be able to raise money, especially if you have a unique new product. In return for a certain contribution, supporters receive products once they finally become available. In essence, these prerelease customers crowdfund the new business. This differs from equity-based crowdfunding, in which many individuals invest small amounts of cash into a new business or product.

Another crowdfunding option that some desperate small businesses have turned to during the pandemic is to appeal to their past customers and supporters to donate to the business through a crowdfunding campaign on a platform such as GoFundMe (www.gofundme.com)

As with other forms of funding, to raise money through crowdfunding, you'll have to do your work. You'll have to spend time (and perhaps some money) driving people to your campaign. You'll have to explain your idea or your situation. And you'll have to convince investors or givers that you'll survive and succeed.

Some crowdfunding sites to check out:

■ **Crowdfunder** (www.crowdfunder.com)

■ **Flashfunders** (www.flashfunders.com)

■ **IndieGoGo** (www.indiegogo.com)

■ **Kickstarter** (www.kickstarter.com)

■ **Republic** (www.republic.co)

■ **SeedInvest** (seedinvest.com)

- **StartEngine** (startengine.com)
- **Wefunder** (wefunder.com)

FREE OR ON THE CHEAP

FREE MONEY. Of the business plan competitions listed below, many are run by universities and are open to students or recent graduates. If you're a little more, let's say mature, but someone on your team fits the competition's entry requirements, you may be eligible to enter your business. Prizes can range from a few thousand to hundreds of thousands of dollars.

- **Harvard Business School New Venture Competition**
  (www.hbs.edu/newventurecompetition/Pages/default.aspx)

- **Hult Prize**
  (www.hultprize.org)

- **Michigan Business Competition**
  (http://zli.umich.edu/programs-funds/michigan-business-challenge)

- **MIT Entrepreneurship Competition**
  (www.mit100k.org)

- **Penn Wharton Awards, Prizes, and Competitions**
  (https://entrepreneurship.wharton.upenn.edu/funding)

- **Postcode Lotteries Green Challenge**
  (www.greenchallenge.info)

- **Rice Business Plan Competition**
  (https://rbpc.rice.edu)

- **U.Pitch**
  (https://futurefounders.com/startup/upitch)

- **Utah Entrepreneur Challenge**
  (https://lassonde.utah.edu/uec)

---

31. Watch out for "fintech" lenders

Over the last decade, recognizing the large number of small businesses that need money, online financing companies jumped in to fill this need. These so-called "fintech" (financial technology) lenders like to emphasize that they are innovative—using different ways to assess a company's credit-worthiness other than just traditional methods. They may access your online accounts, such as your Quickbooks accounts, or they'll check your social media engagement. They'll act fast; you'll get approved or denied within hours, sometimes minutes. That's very attractive.

But beware! With many—if not most—of these fintech lenders, you're likely to pay sky-high interest rates (that won't be apparent to you) and lenders pile on fees (often hidden from you). Whenever possible, rely on traditional lending sources and be very, very careful when dealing with these "innovative" sharks.

THE SH*T'S HIT THE FAN ...

**99 RECESSION-PROOF TIPS FOR
SMALL BUSINESS SUCCESS**

CONNECT
WITH
CUSTOMERS

What you need to know since the sh*t's hit the fan.

Sure, your income took a hit because of the shutdown and subsequent economic downturn—perhaps a huge hit. And sure, the state of the future economy is also uncertain. But there's a long-recognized rule: in down economies, companies that maintain (or even increase) their marketing emerge healthier than companies that cut back their marketing.

After all, now is a time of change. Customers and clients are looking for new, better, more affordable solutions for their needs and wants. Customers' and prospects' normal buying and shopping (and living) patterns have changed. They are open to doing business with new companies. But customers and prospects—just like you—are distracted. That means it's harder for them to remember you or to notice your typical marketing activities.

So now is not the time to cut back your marketing—it's time to step on the gas pedal. And if you always just relied on "word of mouth," now may be when you need to actually put more effort into your marketing and actively getting the word out about your business.

Yes, I know that's a tall order when your bank account may be low and every single penny counts and you're struggling just to keep your business alive. That means you need to find ways to market that are effective in achieving your goals while watching your bottom line like a hawk.

In this section, we'll help you get the most out of every marketing dollar, giving you a whole slew of ideas to help customers know about you, remember you, and spend money with you. Realistically, some of these cost a little bit of money. But marketing is one area that—if you do it wisely—will help you make money.

32. Master marketing basics

Before you spend any money on marketing, it's critical to first figure out what your message is. You need to be able to clearly and quickly explain what you sell, why customers should buy from you, and what action you'd like prospects to take.

Does that seem obvious? You'd be surprised at how many businesspeople overlook some of these basics. It's understandable. After all, you're so used to dealing with the day-to-day aspects of your business that you forget that these basic features may not be obvious to everyone.

The basics: what you sell or do

When someone asks, "What does your company do?" you need a brief, clear answer that quickly sums up the nature of your business. This has to be short! Could you explain your business if you ran into a potential client on an elevator ride in a three-story building? That's why this short description is called the "elevator pitch." If it takes you more than three floors to describe your company, you're saying too much. For social media marketing and other written marketing materials, your description has to be much, much shorter. After all, you don't have "three floors" to describe your business, you just have a few words.

The basics: your competitive advantage

If you're in an easy-to-understand business, your description theoretically could be very short: "I sell real estate." But that doesn't distinguish you from all the other realtors out there. A more memorable elevator pitch sets you apart: "I sell homes in the Lakewood district, specializing in first-time buyers." When you can cut straight to the heart of the matter with what sets you apart, customers immediately understand your benefits. It's like the Vietnamese restaurant I used to go to. I never knew the real name, but always referred to it by the big sign they had out front: "Fresh, Cheap, Good." Now that's a clear message!

The basics: call to action

Prospects and customers won't necessarily know what to do unless you tell them. "Call now for an appointment." "Click to buy a gift card." Almost every marketing activity should have a clear call to action—a straightforward message that asks recipients to take a specific action. Now, you may feel like asking people to "buy now," "click now," feels pushy. It's not. You're in business and they understand that people in business need customers. But, sometimes—not always—you can be a bit gentler with "click here for special deals," or "sign up now to learn more."

Your call to action needs to be:

- **Clear.** Stick to simple words, short phrases.

- **Compelling.** Use action-oriented verbs and phrases: "buy now," "call today," "click here."

- **Rewarding.** Offer an incentive or reward for action. For example, "$100 gift card for only $80 if purchased by Friday," "Act now and also receive..." or "the first 100 respondents will be entered into a raffle to win..."

- **Urgent.** The longer an email sits in an inbox, the less likely it is to be acted on. Create a sense of urgency to get a more immediate response. Try limiting the offer to a specific time period, to the "first 50 customers," "while supplies last," etc.

- **Visible.** Place call-to-action links at various places in your marketing efforts—sometimes the beginning, sometimes the middle, and always again at the end of the email so that prospects can act whenever they are ready.

- **Direct.** Your call-to-action links should go to the appropriate page on your website or social media page, providing customers with your email address, phone number, or other contact information.

The basics: repetition, repetition, repetition.

Hearing or seeing something just once doesn't make an impression. Various studies indicate that a message must be seen or heard at least seven to ten times before someone will recall it. That's just recall—it takes even longer before someone acts on an ad or your social media post and answers your call to action. Think of it this way: Say you're at a party. After you've been introduced to dozens of people, how many names will you remember? Who'll stand out? Chances are, unless a particular person is absolutely fascinating or drop-dead gorgeous, you probably won't remember him. On the other hand, think about the people you see over and over—at your office, at school, or around the neighborhood. You'll soon remember not only their names, but also their faces and personalities and a lot more. Repetition leads to remembering.

QUICK TIP:
Negotiate on advertising prices

Right now, virtually every advertising entity is hurting for customers. That gives you the ability to negotiate prices. You may have difficulty negotiating with social media sites and search engines, but if you're advertising in print, TV, or radio, every media outlet has some unsold space they are likely to sell to smaller advertisers at a fraction of the regular price. In this economic environment, ask for deals!

33. Use visuals

They say an image is worth 1000 words. Well, whether or not that's true, images certainly capture attention. As part of your messaging, you should almost always be including an image. That's true with every kind of marketing piece—emails, brochures, signs—but adding visuals is an absolute must with most social media posts.

Although images are critical to successful social media posts—especially on Instagram—you don't need to be a professional photographer to create great visuals. You can take simple pics or videos with your phone. You'll also find all kinds of free, quality stock images and video in every category possible. And there are free or on-the-cheap apps to help you manipulate those images and add text.

Use your images not only on social media but throughout your business—in email newsletters, on your website, in slide presentations, and so on. Don't worry if you don't have a perfect image or perfect caption. You just want to catch someone's eye. Remember that people scroll through quickly and will spend a fraction of time with your post compared to the time you spent creating it.

Of course, if you have the time to create a high quality video of your products, service, or place of business, that's great. But it's better to have something (as long as it's not offensive) than nothing.

FREE OR ON THE CHEAP

FOR QUALITY STOCK IMAGES, free or very cheap, check sites like **Unsplash** (https://unsplash.com), **Pexels** (www.pexels.com), **and Pixabay** (https://pixabay.com).

After you've downloaded your images, add text and effects with apps like easy-to-use **Canva** (www.canva.com) **on your desktop or Adobe Photoshop Express on your iPhone or Android.**

For quick text overlay, use the apps "Typic" or "Word Swag" for iOS or create collages with Instagram's own app, "Layout." A quick search of photo editing apps will turn up dozens of contenders, many of which are free to use.

34. Emphasize "shop small, shop local"

One thing that is unique about this specific time: customers are eager to support small and local businesses now more than ever. People understand that small businesses have taken a hit during the Covid-19 shutdowns and are struggling through no fault of their own. Customers want to help their local restaurants, bookstores, salons, and gift stores survive. So now is the time to remind them that you're still there and a critical part of their community. There's more about this in the last section, but whenever you're thinking about marketing make the most of the fact that you're a small and local business, a vital part of your community.

Customers feel good about supporting small and local businesses. Yet, they may be able to get something slightly cheaper at a big box or warehouse store or by ordering online, so you need to remind them of why they feel good about purchasing from you. And that means you have to make the fact that you're local and small a part of your marketing efforts.

- **Let customers know you are a small and local business.** Put that on your signs. Put that on your website. Put that in your social media posts. Put that on your take-out bags. Put that message everywhere. It doesn't have to be clever; it just has to be frequent: "Thank you for shopping small, shopping local." "Your dollars support your local community." "We're part of your community, so thank you."

- **Use social media tools for small business.** Instagram and other social media sites have created buttons to call out local and small businesses. Use those buttons yourself and encourage customers to use them too—and be sure to give a call out to other local businesses.

- **Partner with the locals.** Pull together with other local, small businesses and local business organizations, such as business improvement districts, chambers of commerce, or just the small businesses in your same area. Together, you can plan special events or marketing materials and have a better chance of getting local coverage for those activities.

■ **Engage hyper-local media and local websites.** Most communities have small, very local papers. They depend on local businesses for their survival, so stay in touch with them and continually feed them stories about your business, other businesses in your neighborhood, and promotions and events you plan. Also, post promotions on hyper-local websites serving specific neighborhoods, encouraging local residents to shop local.

FREE OR ON THE CHEAP

NEXTDOOR is a widely-used website and app (www.nextdoor.com) where people in very distinct small neighborhoods can share recommendations—especially about services and businesses—get news, ask advice. One specific, stated purpose is "It's where communities come together to keep a local shopkeeper in business." Become a power user of NextDoor to respond to requests and encourage your satisfied customers (and employees) to post about you on NextDoor.

---

35. Get your customer contact list together

For many businesses, the single most important asset they have is their customer and prospect list—their contacts. That's more important now than ever when customers are likely to want to help your business survive and thrive. Only by having a meaningful list of customers and prospects—and their contact information—can you remind people that you are still there doing business and let them know about your products and services.

If you haven't been building your contact list of customers and leads, start today. If you have a list already, now's the time to expand it and update the information. The easiest way to do this is to set up a system to routinely capture and enter data.

Now you may say, "I already have a whole bunch of followers on my social media channels. Why do I need my own contact list?" One simple answer: *YOU* OWN YOUR CONTACT LIST; *SOCIAL MEDIA COMPANIES* OWN YOUR FOLLOWERS.

Yep—all those followers you have on Facebook, Instagram, Twitter, LinkedIn, YouTube, whatever—those companies control how and when you reach your followers and how much you'll pay to do so. They can change the rules at any time. They can charge you to reach them. They could start purging them. Those names are theirs—not yours.

So start building your own contact list and keep building it. With your contact list, you can reach your contacts through email, through texts, through phone calls, through regular mail—through whatever kind of contact information you have.

Always be collecting contact information from your customers and prospects using some of the following techniques:

- **Ask.** The simplest way to capture contacts is to ask. Ask anyone who comes to your place of business, to your website, or through your social media channels for their contact info. The two most important pieces of info to gather: their email addresses and their names. You might also want to get their social media handles, and if they'll let you, their phone numbers to receive texts. Train employees to invite customers to sign up too.

■ **Offer an incentive.** People are more likely to give you their contact info if they have an incentive. Do something as simple and straightforward as having a "Sign up for discounts" or, better yet, "15% off your first order when you join our mailing list."

■ **Tell them why they're signing up.** Let them know they'll get notices of sales, discounts, new products, and "family and friends" specials. Everyone likes a deal.

■ **Hold contests.** Most people love the chance to win something and will gladly enter their names and contact information if there's an enticing prize. The prize doesn't have to cost you a lot—if you own a restaurant, it can be a free dessert or dinner; if you sell a product or service, you can give one of your products or services away or an enhancement to an existing product or services. Just be sure to let them know they'll be added to your contact list.

36. Send out an email newsletter

If you have contact information for your customers and prospects, now is the time to get in touch with them and stay in front of them. In this economic environment, this is a really important thing to do and do regularly. The easiest, fastest way to do that is to send an email newsletter.

While we're going to use the term "newsletter" here, what we're talking about is really using any kind of email marketing. A newsletter can be something as simple as a discount coupon, announcement of a sale, introduction of a new menu item or product or service, or a few tips relating to your product or service. You can just have a "deal of the week" and call that a newsletter. Of course, if you have the time and ability to write a bit more, with more advice and guidance relating to your products or services, people will value that too. In my company, for example, we email a monthly newsletter with use-it-now tips for small-business owners. Sign up for my newsletter at www.PlanningShop.com (see that call to action?).

Do people get tired of email? Yes. Do people only open about one out of every five or so emails they get from a business? Yes. Will some people unsubscribe? Yes.

But will regular emails keep your name in front of prospects? Yes. Will it encourage some people to buy? Yes. Will it help people remember your name to give for referrals? Yes. Are emails fairly easy and cheap to do? Yes.

Try to use a compelling subject line to increase the chance that people will open and read your mail. And make sure your mailings are meaningful, valuable, and free of offensive content or language. If not, recipients will soon block your email, and if enough people do that, email filters may block your messages.

When planning your email campaigns, send email only to those who've signed up to receive email from you or have had some dealings with you (including giving you their business card), or you may be breaking the law. Limit the frequency of your messages; generally once or twice a month is enough and more than once a week is too much.

FREE OR ON THE CHEAP

EMAIL NEWSLETTERS. Many companies provide easy-to-use, turnkey online email newsletter services to help you create and send email newsletters in a snap. Some of them are even free for small mailing lists. Here's a short list:

- **AWeber** (www.aweber.com)

- **Campaign Monitor** (www.campaignmonitor.com)

- **Constant Contact** (www.constantcontact.com)

- **Emma** (www.myemma.com)

- **JangoMail** (www.jangomail.com)

- **MailChimp** (www.mailchimp.com)

- **Vertical Response** (www.verticalresponse.com)

NOW WHAT?!

37. Create a customer loyalty program

People love getting something free. You want your customers coming back. The perfect solution to both those desires? A customer loyalty program. After all, it pays to take care of your best customers: those who purchase frequently or are highly profitable. And good customers want to feel valued by a business. Customer loyalty programs are designed to do exactly that.

The most obvious example of these programs is airline frequent flyer programs—those programs often keep customers choosing airlines even when the flights may be more expensive or less convenient. But even a simple coffee shop "punch card" keeps customers coming back to get that 10th cup of coffee free.

Now it's easier than ever to have a loyalty program. Many "POS"—point-of-sale—programs like Square (https://squareup.com/us/en), credit card acceptance apps, and website programs (such as Wordpress) have built-in loyalty applications or add-ons, and you can also find many loyalty program apps to use for your business. Check with your industry association for reward programs best suited to your type of business or just search for "loyalty card app for small business."

Loyalty programs keep customers attached to you, and they all have some basic attributes in common:

- **Reward.** The customer gets a reward for being a regular or big customer.

- **Tracking.** A good loyalty program provides a way to keep track of customers' purchases.

- **Contact.** Customers usually provide their contact information, which the business can then use to keep marketing to them.

Types of loyalty programs

- **Membership or clubs:** Discounts or rewards for people who agree to sign up to be a member of your club or be associated with you.

■ **Free reward after multiple purchases:** Enticing customers to keep coming back to you by offering them something free after they make a certain number of purchases.

■ **Buy-ahead discounts:** A significant discount or freebie for buying multiple products or services in advance.

■ **Upgrades or special services:** A special treatment or better product offered at no extra charge for repeat customers.

■ **Discounts after purchase:** Discounts given as a reward after purchase, which can be used in the future.

Stay Sane:
Stay Off Your Phone

Yes, social media may work for your small business. But beware! Social media can ruin your productivity. Limit the amount of time you allow yourself to spend posting, commenting, liking, and sharing so you can get to the crucial work that actually pays the bills. Productivity apps like Forest (www.forestapp.cc) and Freedom (https://freedom.to) help prevent you from checking your social media sites on your phone every 10 minutes.

38. Develop a social media following

While it is critical to own your own contact list, having an engaged social media following can also be a meaningful way to connect with customers and prospects, especially if you have a product or service that people are likely to buy directly from a social media feed, such as fitness, beauty, or fashion products.

Social media has proven to be a game changer in small business marketing. Many—most?—people look at their social media feeds regularly, often many times a day. So having a popular social media following means you can stay in front of customers and prospects in a place they're already looking.

But social media—done right—takes time, both time in your busy weekly schedule and time to build an audience. Many—most?—small businesses get frustrated with their social media attempts because the time it takes does not immediately pay off in terms of direct sales. You may find you need to assign or hire a staff member (or get a family member) to manage your social media—posting frequently—unless you personally really like posting to social media.

One of the first things you need to determine is which social media platforms best suit your target market. Are you trying to reach consumers or businesses? Does a mass-market site (Facebook, Instagram, Twitter, YouTube, TikTok), a professional networking site (like LinkedIn), or a special interest site (such as Houzz for home improvement, Pinterest for consumer products, Chowhound for food) best suit your offerings and your audience? Before launching a social media campaign, be certain that the site's audience is the right fit for your offerings.

Once you've identified the most appropriate social media sites, the key to your marketing campaign's success will be providing content that appeals to your target audience—FREQUENTLY. Posting once or twice a month won't cut it. You have to be a presence in your prospects' feeds.

With so many interactive online marketing tools to consider, how do you choose the right one for you?

■ **Listen before you speak.** Make sure your target market actually follows and participates in the social media platform you're choosing. Closely follow and participate in the community before you decide to spend a great deal of time and/or money on any particular site.

■ **Weigh the time factor.** Do you have the time for "unpaid" social media? Are you willing to develop and maintain an active online presence? If you lack the time, then pay for ads online—they can be persistent even when you can't.

■ **Measure the risks.** Understand that online activities can come with pitfalls. Most notably, dissatisfied customers may make unfavorable comments—not all of them even fair or honest—about your products, services, or customer service.

FREE OR ON THE CHEAP

SOCIAL MEDIA MANAGEMENT TOOLS. Make your social media campaigns more efficient with free management tools. Hootsuite (www.hootsuite.com) and Buffer (https://buffer.com) allow you to pre-load and schedule posts, and follow activity on your various social media platforms. Both offer free basic versions and paid versions with more features. The free app Tweetdeck (www.tweetdeck.com) helps you manage Twitter.

---

39. Advertise on social media

Remember, while social media companies like to tout themselves as communication platforms, they are really only advertising platforms. As such, you'll likely find it takes quite a while to reach enough people through social media organically—just through creating engaging posts—to make a significant difference in your business right now. Social media companies want you to pay to get seen.

As an advertising platform, social media channels have proven to be very useful. You can be HIGHLY selective in who you target to see your posts/ads. On a site like Facebook or Instagram, you can narrow in on a specific zipcode and specific interests. For instance, if you own a seafood restaurant, you could choose to have your "posts" (think of them as ads, not posts) reach people in your target zipcode, who like to eat out, and who like seafood. On LinkedIn, you could target people in certain areas and specific industries with specific titles. There are almost no other advertising options that are so targeted.

You still have to put time and effort in, however, even if you're paying for "eyeballs." You need to make your posts engaging—with visuals, a compelling message, and a clear call to action. Many social media sites have tools to help you get viewers to take a specific action, such as a "buy now" or "learn more" button to get to your website.

If you do spend money on social media ads, experiment! Try a few different posts with different offers/calls to action to see which get the best response. Then repeat those that are the most successful.

40. Optimize your website for search engines

For many small businesses, search engines bring far greater traffic to their websites than social media. That's because for the vast majority of online users, search engines serve as the main gateway to information online.

And right now, you want to be seen when someone is looking for a business like yours in a geographic area like yours. Now is a good time to take a look at your website and make sure it's optimized so that prospects and customers can find you.

There are two primary ways to ensure that your website is highly visible on search engines. **Search engine optimization** (SEO)—otherwise known as "organic search"—and **search engine marketing** (SEM). SEM refers to the process of paying search engine companies to ensure that your website appears in users' search results. You want to get as many results free, of course.

The first thing you need to do is figure out which words your target customers will most likely use when searching for the types of products or services (or content) you offer. Once you've determined that, repeat those keywords throughout your site—in your content, headlines, page names, and more. Use the free tools below to help you achieve those results.

FREE OR ON THE CHEAP

SEO HELP. Do a search for "Google SEO Starter Guide" to find a link to a document full of basic information on SEO, including getting your site on Google, structuring your website, guidance on finding an SEO specialist if you'd prefer to pay someone to optimize your site for you, and more. (https://support.google.com/webmasters/answer/7451184?hl=en)

Google Analytics (www.google.com/analytics) **analyzes how many people are visiting your site and gives you an impressive array of information about them, such as what pages they are viewing, how long they view them, at what point they abandon your site, and so forth. It's extremely versatile and offers a broad array of reports to help you make changes in your site to improve your results. The basic version is free.**

You'll need to choose relevant keywords for your business for both SEO and SEM. A good place to start is with Google's free keyword tool (https://adwords.google.com/home/tools/keyword-planner).

41. "Claim" your business

Here's a free way to advertise and get found that many small businesses overlook: "claiming" their business on search engines and review sites. This is easy, free, quick, and really important. And it's a critically important way to help customers and prospects find you.

By claiming your business, you are giving a search engine (such as Google) and review sites (such as Yelp) more information to share with users. This is particularly important for local retail, restaurant, and service businesses. And the more local you are, the more important claiming your business is.

Say, for instance, a user searches for a yogurt shop in Los Gatos, California or a plumber in Brentwood, Tennessee on Google or on Google maps. That searcher can find hours of service, pictures, menus, types of services, delivery options, and more for those companies that have claimed their businesses and provided information. And their information is likely to be more prominently displayed.

This is free advertising that you should definitely take advantage of. Be sure to look for ways to claim your business on:

- **Google My Business** (www.google.com/business)

- **Bing Places** (www.bingplaces.com)

- **Yahoo Local** (https://smallbusiness.yahoo.com/local)

- **Yelp** (https://biz.yelp.com/support/claiming)

- **American Express** (www.americanexpress.com/ShopSmallMap)

42. Keep your customers happy

Successful marketing involves not just getting customers but also keeping them. It can cost from two to ten times more to acquire a customer than it does to retain one. For example, it costs far less to send a monthly email to a past customer than it does to buy social media ads to attract new customers.

Moreover, the longer a customer remains with you and continues to buy, the more profitable the relationship. And the more they like you, the more likely they are to refer others to you. That's why it pays to treat customers as the valuable entities they are.

What keeps customers coming back? Of course, you need to offer an excellent product or service at a competitive price. But you must also be seen as responsive, polite, and attentive. If they have a problem, you need to show you are trying to fix it. If they complain, the worse thing you can do is ignore the complaint.

Right now, with customers feeling stressed, you and your employees may find that some customers are rude to you and your staff, especially if you have to enforce health guidelines.

The important thing is to just continue to be polite, regardless of how rude or belligerent the customer may become. Train EVERY employee to be courteous and responsive. Remember, today, not only can customers ding you on review sites for bad service, they can whip out their phones and post videos.

Of course, if a customer is offensive, you can ask them to leave your place of business; just have everyone on your staff continue to keep their cool.

Get the basics right: deliver what you promise, on time, or stay in touch if there's a problem. Respond to inquiries. Say hello to everyone coming in your place of business. Say thank you. And go the extra mile by occasionally adding an unexpected benefit, such as giving a diner a free dessert for their birthday or washing the customer's car after an oil change.

NOW WHAT?!

43. Remember to use signs

This may seem incredibly obvious, but if you have a physical place of business—a brick-and-mortar store, restaurant, spa, etc.—signs are one of the most effective, least expensive ways to get the word out about your business and products and services.

Signs come in all forms and sizes, from a billboard in Times Square, to the name of your construction company on the side of your truck, to a "sandwich" sign on the corner pointing passers-by to your establishment. They can be inside or outside your place of business: a banner inside your store—saying you cater, deliver, sell cheese, whatever—brings attention to what you want to sell. Signs get people's attention.

Besides being pretty darn cheap, signs are persistent. They stay in one place for a long time, unlike an ad that disappears in 30 seconds or a social media posting that gets overlooked immediately. You can even have employees' t-shirts (or face masks?) be a sign with a company message ("Ask me about free delivery").

NOW WHAT?!

44. Create and send out press releases

Right now the media—especially local media—is particularly interested in stories about small business, particularly local businesses. This gives you an opportunity to get some of the best advertising there is—free. A story in a local paper, on a local TV or radio station, or on a popular website can be much more powerful than a paid advertisement.

To get that coverage, however, you usually have to reach out to the media yourself or through a PR agency (which can cost a lot of money). So you'll need to learn to do your own press releases and how to follow up.

A press release is a document that provides the media with a story hook: "After Covid, this store has re-invented customer service" or "How this local graphic design firm created online 'brainstorming sessions' in their new work-from-home world."

It's not just enough to send out a press release. You have to follow up with the media—through emails, calls, texts—to remind them of your information.

What to include in a press release

■ All the info that a media representative needs to write a story about the event, product, service, and so on, including all the details (dates, names, prices—whatever is relevant).

■ Quotations for the media writer to use. These quotes might come from customers praising the product or service, a local or industry specialist, or a representative of the company.

■ Graphics, videos, and website links if you have them.

■ Contact info that the media can use to get further information.

NOW WHAT?!

45. Consider traditional print, radio, and TV ads

If you can afford it, don't overlook the most time-honored way of getting the word out about your business—advertising in traditional media: newspapers, magazines, radio, and TV. Just because this form of advertising has been around for a long time doesn't mean it should be dismissed. It has stuck around for a reason: It works.

This kind of media advertising is effective at reaching both a large mainstream audience (think of the reach of a Super Bowl commercial, for example) and a highly targeted selection of consumers (for instance, a hyper-local newspaper, an industry publication, a magazine appealing to wine drinkers). For most small businesses—especially retail, restaurants, personal services, and real estate—hyper-local and local newspapers and websites are the most effective.

To advertise effectively in these traditional venues, you need to find out which media attracts the attention of your target market—that is, what sections of the newspaper they read, what magazines they subscribe to, what radio stations and programs they listen to, and what channels their TVs are tuned to—and then present your message there as often as your company can afford.

Of course, this kind of advertising can be expensive. And it has to be repeated over and over and over and over again to be effective. So do your research before you plunge in because, in these uncertain economic times, every dollar counts.

THE SH*T'S HIT THE FAN ...

NOW
WHAT?!

99 RECESSION-PROOF TIPS FOR
SMALL BUSINESS SUCCESS

MAKE SALES

What you need to know since the sh*t's hit the fan.

Even if everything in your small business has changed significantly due to the economic downturn—perhaps you adapted your business model, had to close for a long period, or relocated your company from a physical location to a virtual one online—one thing remains the same: Sales are the heart of your business. And you need to take care of that heart. Whether your business needs a quadruple bypass to save its life or merely a daily aspirin for preventative care, in this section of *Now What?* we'll come up with a prescription to help you keep your business healthy by getting more money into your bank account the best way possible: making sales.

46. Call on your existing customers

First things first: Sell to your present and past customers.

When the economy goes south, many small businesses scramble to find new customers. That, of course, makes sense. You need more people buying from you.

But while new customers are always necessary, acquiring them can cost from two to 10 times more than retaining existing customers. Just think how much less it costs to send a monthly email to a current or past customer than it does to buy social media ads to attract new customers.

Sure, you may lose some, if not many, of your current and past customers as their lives and needs change in response to the economic, social, and health conditions. But if you're looking for sales, the first place to look for revenue is from people who've already opened their wallets to you before.

In these turbulent times, your customers have been consumed with their own lives, so they may have forgotten about you. It's important for you to remind your past customers that you're still around and still available to meet their needs.

The longer a customer remains with you and continues to buy, the more profitable the relationship. That's why it pays to reward customer loyalty and keep customers with you as long as possible.

So be sure to call on your existing customers *before* you look for new ones, especially if you're making any special offers.

Here's your do-it-now action item: Make a list of your best customers and reach out to them this week. Send an email, pick up the phone and make a call, or send a text. Don't make this a "hard sell" contact. Ask them how they're doing, find out what they need, determine their priorities in this new environment, and let them know you appreciate them and their business. And let them know that your business is still there for them and tell them about any changes you've made.

NOW WHAT?!

47. Expand how you think about making sales

How will you sell your product or service? Seems a simple question, doesn't it? But there are lots of different ways to get money coming into your business from sales.

For instance, a restaurant owner might answer that question just by saying: "People will walk into my establishment, and I'll sell them prepared meals."

But think about the other ways people could buy prepared meals from that restaurant owner:

■ Order take-out from restaurant's website

■ Buy gift cards off restaurant's website

■ Buy gift cards or order take-out from ads on social media

■ Order take-out from online restaurant delivery services

But let's help that restaurant owner think about some of the many other ways to make sales:

■ Make cold calls on surrounding businesses to sell their catering services

■ Sell subscriptions for customers to receive weekly/monthly meals

■ Sell subscriptions for customers to receive regular "meal preparation kits" for customers to cook at home

■ Set up a stand/booth for pick-up of packaged prepared meals from the outdoor dining area/public places/festivals

So, as you start to think about how to make more money in your business, consider some of the many ways you can make sales, including:

■ **Direct sales:** an end-use customer buys directly from you without any intermediary

■ **Ecommerce:** customers buy from your website

■ **Platform sales:** customers buy your products online from another website

■ **Wholesale:** customers who plan to re-sell your products buy from you at large discounts

■ **Distributor:** another company sells your products to others and takes a percentage of the sale or a fee

■ **Social media sales:** you sell from your social media presence

■ **Subscription sales:** a customer pays an ongoing fee to get your products or services on a regular basis

■ **Membership:** a customer pays a fee to join and receive certain perks, such as discounts or special treatment

■ **Licensing:** you are paid to allow your name to be used by another company on its products or services

■ **"White labeling":** you make a product or service that others market under their own brand

NOW WHAT?!

48. Attract your first customers

In response to changing conditions, perhaps you've started a new line of business. Or perhaps you've just launched a new business. Either way, you may not have any customers yet for your new endeavor. How do you attract and land your first customers?

While the Starship Enterprise may go "where no one has gone before," most customers only follow where others lead. Most people hate to be the first to try something. Customers generally prefer to patronize companies that already have other customers. What a dilemma. You have to have customers to get customers.

Don't despair! There are a couple of tried-and-true tricks for snagging that first customer:

- **Give it away.** The simplest method is to just give your product or service away. This isn't as stupid as it sounds. Technology companies often give potential customers "beta" or test versions of their software. They use this as a way both to improve their product and to expose future buyers to what they make. Food product producers give away massive amounts of "samples" to get customers to taste the product for the first time. Of course, for small businesses giving away a lot of your product or service can be costly, but consider ways that you can let potential customers "sample" your offerings.

- **Charge much less—for now.** Another approach is to simply be a much better bargain. You charge early clients far less than they would pay elsewhere (and less than you'll charge later). How do you charge less now and raise the price later? Lots of companies use "introductory pricing" for their products or services to start to build market share. This enables you to start building customer loyalty as well as gaining positive reviews and customer stories. It also helps you build testimonials and word-of-mouth advertising. Use community and social media to help get the word out.

49. Offer gift cards and pre-payment options

Once upon a time, gift certificates were just that: paper "certificates" that were bought to be given as "gifts." But while the name may have only slightly changed—from "gift certificate" to "gift card"—the purpose of gift cards are much broader than "gifts" and they're often not even "cards." So don't let the name fool you.

"Gift cards" are—quite simply—a way for customers to give you money for something they—or someone else—may (or may not) buy in the future. Gift cards are a critical tool for most small businesses. It's time you figure out how to implement one in your company.

Here's the best way to think of "gift cards"—they're interest-free loans from a customer that you only have to pay back with goods or services, not cash. And here's even better news: a portion of those loans will NEVER have to be paid back, as many people never actually use all or some of the value of their pre-purchases.

And it's now a snap to offer gift cards, especially if you use some kind of "POS" (Point-of-Sale) or ecommerce checkout provider or your website (or ecommerce portion of your website) is hosted by a marketplace ecommerce company, such as Shopify (www.shopify.com), Wix (www.wix.com), BigCommerce (www.bigcommerce.com), Squarespace (www.squarespace.com) and so on. Many have built-in gift card/prepayment options, and it just takes a few clicks to turn on "egift card" functionality that seamlessly integrates with your existing purchasing system. If you don't have such a system, there are "plug-ins" for your website—ask your web developer to help you with them.

Yes, you might have to pay a small amount to some gift card providers, but they're well worth it. Why?

■ **You get the money NOW, not later.** Remember, money in the bank is ALWAYS better than money you might—or might not—get later. When a customer purchases a gift card, you've got that money to use NOW.

■ **Customers spend more.** Studies have shown that recipients of gift cards tend to spend more—a lot more—than the gift cards face value. Almost 60% of gift card recipients spend more than the amount of the gift they receive.

■ **Customers don't use all the money on the card.** There's a good chance that a portion—perhaps as much as 10-20%—of the gift card sales you make will never be redeemed. Wow! That means more money for you!

■ **People like buying gift cards.** The easiest gift for someone to give—especially if they've waited til the last minute—is a gift card. It's an impulse buy and it solves a problem for the person who doesn't know what to give as a present. And more and more, people like buying gift cards—or pre-purchase options—for themselves, especially if it's in the form of a digital purchase that stays on their phone, making it easier for them to use.

■ **People like getting gift cards.** For more than 13 years, gift cards were the number one most preferred holiday gift.

■ **You find new customers.** When someone gives a gift card from your business to a friend or family member who's never been a customer before, it's a terrific way to build a new relationship.

For you, as a business, offering gift cards is a good way to serve your customers, get money now, increase the amount and value of sales, and build loyalty from and with your customers. If you don't currently offer gift cards—especially egift cards—it's time to do it now.

50. Find sales leads

To make a sale, first identify potential customers—or leads. A good lead can become a buyer if that person or company has the need or interest in your product or service, the finances to purchase, and can be reached with your message.

There are three basic kinds of leads:

■ **Hot leads.** These highly desirable prospects are the most likely to convert to a sale; typically, they've shown interest in your offering and are clearly ready to purchase. For example, if you sell cars, a hot lead is the person who walks onto your lot and says, "My car's broken down, can't be fixed, and I have to get to work."

■ **Qualified leads.** These prospects have the interest and wherewithal to purchase what you sell. For example, if you sell new BMWs and a prospect arrives in a used BMW, they're probably qualified to buy a new one (not guaranteed, of course), although they may not necessarily be ready to buy—in other words, they may not be "hot."

■ **Cold leads.** These are names and contacts you get from other sources. These may or may not have a strong interest or need for your product or service, nor are they necessarily qualified to purchase. However, cold leads often do convert to paying customers, and therefore much of selling involves reaching out to cold leads.

How do you get leads? It's possible to buy lists—such as purchasers of related products, past attendees of trade shows, users of certain websites. For instance, if you sell SUVs, you can purchase a list of new mothers or pregnant women from a local hospital (and yes, they do sell such lists!), on the assumption that growing families need larger cars.

You can also get leads from social media sites such as Facebook. They don't provide you with lists and contact information, but you can target specific audiences with your paid ads that direct people to "buy."

NOW WHAT?!

51. Develop successful sales techniques

Whether or not you consider yourself a salesperson, when you're in business, sooner or later you'll personally have to make sales, and you'll certainly hire people to make sales for you. Some entrepreneurs view the prospect of a sales call with the same sense of fear and loathing as having to face an IRS audit. Take heart: Sales is a craft, not an art. It can be learned. Here are some keys to successful sales:

■ **Listen.** No sales skill is more important than the ability to listen. A great salesperson hears what the customer wants—their concerns and priorities. When calling on a customer, it's tempting to immediately launch into a sales pitch, especially if you're nervous. But by listening, you can better understand how your product or service meets the customer's needs and desires. If a woman shopping for a car says she likes to drive fast, tell her about performance instead of cup holders. If a man is concerned about safety, focus on the airbags and antilock brakes. Don't just tell the customer what you think they'll be interested in or stick to your standard sales patter.

■ **Ask questions.** You can't listen to a customer unless you get them talking. Ask relevant questions to draw them out: "What do you like in your current car?" "What don't you like?" "What features are the most important?" Don't just ask questions to qualify them as a hot prospect, such as, "Are you ready to buy a car today?"

■ **Tell them what they get, not what you do.** You work with your product or service every day, so it's natural to focus on details of your work. But customers don't want to know the ins and outs of your business; they want to know how you meet their needs.

■ **Appreciate the benefits of your product or service.** Genuine enthusiasm is contagious. If you truly believe you're offering the customer something worthwhile, you'll be a more effective salesperson. On the other hand, if you don't believe in your product, you shouldn't be selling it.

■ **Don't oversell.** It's tempting to land a sale by telling the customer anything they want to hear, but that's almost certain to lead to customers' being dissatisfied or disappointed. An owner of a chain of very successful moderately priced hotels said his strategy was to "promise customers a Chevy, then deliver a Cadillac." By under-promising and over-delivering, he built an exceptionally loyal customer base and a large hotel chain.

■ **Be honest.** Lying is not only unethical and possibly illegal, it's a surefire way to lose customers and potential customers. You may even find yourself facing a lawsuit.

■ **Compare, don't criticize, your competition.** Yes, sure, your product or service is so much better than your competitor's, and they're really not very nice people either. But disparaging your competition makes you appear malicious. Instead, factually—and positively—compare your benefits and value to those of your competitor.

■ **Build relationships.** One of Rhonda's Rules is "people do business with other people." We all prefer to do business with people we like and trust. Consider the "lifetime value" of a customer, not just a onetime sale. Often, you might want to make a little less profit to begin an ongoing customer relationship. Get to know your customers; find out about their businesses or families. One way for small businesses to compete with the big guys is by building strong customer relationships.

52. Polish your sales pitch

You've listened and you've asked the right questions. It's time to make the pitch—to actually ask a prospective customer to buy your product or service.

A sales pitch can come in many forms, but basically, there are four parts:

- **Your pitch.** The old rule about a sales pitch was "sell benefits not features." In other words, concentrate on how your product or service benefits the customer. Remember, you've *listened* first, so you know what's important to the prospect. You might also need to include the key things that distinguish you from your competition.

- **The customer's concerns and objections.** Allow time for the prospect to ask you questions and raise their issues. You WANT them to voice their hesitation so that you can address them now and get them to say yes.

- **Your response to those concerns and objections.** Anticipate what concerns might arise so you are prepared to address them in a way that convinces your prospect to buy.

- **Your ask.** This may seem like the hard part, but it's the core of your sales pitch. You have to tell the customer what you're asking from them—to make a purchase, how much it costs, and so on. Don't get into the nitty gritty details—such as shipping, delivery, etc. (unless those are benefits) until after they've said yes.

After you've been in business for a while, you'll know the objections or concerns that keep most prospects from making the decision to buy. Work on those, so you sound confident in responding to them should they arise in the course of a sales call.

It's generally best to anticipate objections and respond to them before they're even raised. This way, you can address whatever shortcomings or problems the prospect may be thinking about but doesn't want to mention out loud.

53. Figure out ways to up-sell and cross-sell

Getting customers isn't cheap. It takes money and time to attract new customers. Perhaps you advertise, buy search engine ads, send direct mail, attend trade shows. You put a lot of effort into getting each customer to walk through your door, call you on the phone, or visit your website, and it costs you the same amount of money whether that customer then spends $1 or $1,000. So it's far more profitable if you can make a bigger sale to each customer who comes your way.

Up-selling and cross-selling increase your sales while, typically, providing your customers with better value. These strategies enable you to provide deals to your customers without having to slash your prices.

Up-selling

Upselling is when you entice a customer who originally wanted to buy something at a lower price point to make a larger buy—often by being offered a good deal on something related to their original intended purchase.

Here's an example of simple up-selling. Let's say a shopper is looking for a new eyeshadow at a beauty supply store. The shopper finds an eyeshadow for $8. Then, the nice salesperson advises the shopper—in a very low-key manner—of a much better deal: they're running a special: For $25, they get three eye shadows and a lipstick. That seems to be a lot better deal.

When up-selling is done properly, the customer gets a good deal and you get a bigger sale. How could the retailer afford this kind of offer? Because its big expense is tied up in overhead—rent, salaries, advertising—not in the cost of the eye shadow.

Up-selling doesn't just occur in retail. If you need to get a will drawn up, don't be surprised if your lawyer offers you a complete estate planning package, which includes a few other documents you should properly prepare at the same time. The one-price package is a good value to you and a better sale for them.

Cross-selling

A slightly different approach is "cross-selling"—selling related products or services at the same time someone is purchasing a different product.

You're probably already used to seeing an example of cross-selling when you buy something on many ecommerce websites. As you hone in on a product, you're likely to see something like "Customers who bought this, also bought these..." That's a very powerful phrase, and it's something you can use even when you're selling in person or otherwise not online.

One time-honored way to cross-sell is to sell products related to a service. For example, hair salons make up to 25% of their income by selling hair care products like shampoo. Gyms often sell work-out clothes.

Of course, there's a risk that if you're too aggressive when you up-sell or cross-sell, customers will be put off. But if you can honestly provide a more complete product or service or a better value by up-selling or cross-selling, both you and your customer will benefit.

STAY SANE!

Stay Legal!

While up-selling and cross-selling are legal sales techniques, "bait-and-switch" methods are illegal in most states and under some federal laws. "Bait and switch" is the practice of using an advertisement or promotion to lure a customer (the "bait") but when the customer requests the promoted item, the salesperson tells them that it is unavailable or inappropriate for their needs and suggests a more expensive option (the "switch"). If you use a low-cost promotion to bring in customers, make certain you have reasonable quantities available and be careful not to be too aggressive in suggesting other, more expensive products instead.

54. Follow up!

Keep in mind that even when there's a robust economy, it can take many months and many contacts to close a sale. And that may be even more true in a recessionary economy. People are pre-occupied and may be slower to get back to you—if they get back to you at all.

Continue to check in on your customers and prospects. Until you hear a solid "No, I don't want to buy your product or service," contact them regularly and try not to get discouraged by a lengthy, extended sales cycle.

FREE OR ON THE CHEAP

ONLINE BOOKING APPS. If you run a service business, make it easy for clients to schedule appointments with you by accepting bookings through an online booking service. Some include:

■ **Square Appointments** (https://squareup.com/appointments)

■ **Accuity Scheduling** (https://acuityscheduling.com)

■ **Setmore** (www.setmore.com)

■ **Gigabook** (https://gigabook.com)

■ **You Can Book Me** (https://youcanbook.me)

■ **MindBody** (www.mindbodyonline.com)

NOW WHAT?!

55. Experiment with pricing

"How much should I charge?" That's one of the toughest questions when you're pivoting to a new line of business or launching a new business. It can be particularly tough when yours is a service business ("should I charge $50 for a haircut or $150?"), but even when selling a product, determining the right amount to charge is challenging.

Setting prices is more of an art than a craft. So how do you know where to set your prices when you've never sold that product or service before?

- **Do your research.** Know what's happening in your market before you set your initial prices. If you sell a product, be sure to check prices online as well as in brick-and-mortar stores. In service businesses, call around so you understand the prices competitors will offer your prospective customers. After all, if the upholstery store across town reupholsters sofas for $500, it will be tough to charge $2,000.

- **Test the market.** Don't take the existing pricing structure for granted. There might be a reason for you to charge four times as much as your nearest competitor—your upholstery shop, for instance, might offer higher grades of fabric or better workmanship. Alternatively, you might find that lowering your prices—charging $300 for the same type of upholstery service—enables you to quickly capture a lot of customers.

- **Offer different price points.** One way to both test the market and reach more customers is to offer different pricing levels. Consider how you can offer "small, medium, large" versions. Most online services already do this with three levels of service. Try this in your business, too. For example, a wedding videographer could offer a "standard" service taking photos at the wedding; "pro" would include post-production editing, and "premium" would include advanced editing and creation of a deluxe wedding album.

■ **Test different prices.** One thing you can do as you first introduce a new product or service is test out some different prices. A good way to do this is online—by placing search or social media ads that are similar except for the price and see what kind of results you get.

Remember: Customers will often pay more, for the same or very similar product, depending on a number of factors, including:

■ **Brand**. Brands enhance customers' familiarity and comfort level with your products and services. In small businesses, the company's reputation may be thought of as their brand.

■ **Convenience.** You can often charge more when you make it more convenient for the customer—better location, delivery, faster service, and so on.

■ **Word of mouth.** Prospects trust referrals from people they know. You're far more likely to go to the restaurant, hire the plumber, or download the app that a friend recommends to you.

■ **Specialization.** If you are seen as someone with particular expertise or knowledge, you can charge more. Targeting a niche market—such as an industry or demographic group—and learning their specific needs enables you to get higher prices.

Remember, setting prices isn't an exact science. So don't be surprised if it takes you a while to figure out what's the "just right" amount to charge.

56. Prepare bids or proposals

In many businesses, bids or proposals are a large part of the sales process. Whether it be bidding on putting in a new deck on a consumer's home, providing equipment for a new production plant, maintaining software for a company, or performing many other services or providing many other products, your bid or proposal may determine whether you'll get the job.

Bids and proposals can be tremendously challenging to develop—especially for newer companies or new lines of business or for new important customers. You want to make sure you're profitable, yet you want to get the job, and that often means being very competitive on price. Often, you may not know all the variables that may affect your costs.

Many entrepreneurs find the hardest part of developing a proposal is figuring out what to charge. You may want to work on a ***project basis*** rather than charge ***an hourly rate***. That way you don't have to keep an eye on the clock every time a client calls, and the client isn't surprised by a big bill at the end of a project. But first make a detailed list of each step to anticipate and figure out how much time it will take and what resources you'll need. That will help you know what to charge to make a fair profit.

There are ways to make writing proposals easier and landing clients more likely. The first trick is to create a template. Develop a standard format (or formats if you prepare more than one type of proposal frequently) so you don't start from scratch every time.

Here's what you may want to include in your proposal template:

■ **Background.** A brief statement of the problem. This basically restates how your potential client has described their situation and lets them know you understand why they're undertaking the project.

■ **Scope.** This is a fairly detailed description of what you are going to do for the client so there can be no misunderstandings later. Be specific!

■ **Deliverables.** If you're creating tangible items for the client—such as writing a report or designing a brochure—list exactly what you'll be giving the client.

■ **Personnel.** Indicate who will be staffing the project and their qualifications. In many cases, this may be you alone, but in others you may have staff or subcontractors who should also be indicated, especially if they add strength to the proposal.

■ **Timetable.** State when the project will start, when certain milestones will be reached, when the project will be considered finished.

■ **Fees.** Clearly state how much you are charging for the project, which expenses are included, whether there is an allowance for possible overcharges and all other fees.

■ **Equipment, outside contractors, and other expenses.** If the project entails other major expenses—such as equipment rental, hiring outside contractors, printing costs—describe who will be responsible for engaging/supervising these services and how they will be billed.

■ **Terms.** Detail when payments are due, how expenses that are not part of the project fees will be billed (at cost, cost plus 10%), what happens when payments are late (amount of interest charged, work stops, and so on).

FREE OR ON THE CHEAP

ELECTRONIC SIGNATURE APPS. Not meeting clients in person? They can still sign on the dotted line so you can close those deals. The following digital signature apps have basic, free versions, with paid premium versions that offer more features:

■ **Docusign** (www.docusign.com)

■ **Eversign** (https://eversign.com)

■ **PandaDoc** (www.pandadoc.com/free-electronic-signature-software)

■ **Hello Sign** (www.hellosign.com)

■ **Docsketch** (www.docsketch.com)

NOW
WHAT?!

57. Make cold calls

After you get leads, it's time to get out there and make sales. That probably means making the most intimidating, most hated kind of sales call: the cold call.

What exactly is a "cold call?" It's a sales call—on the phone or in person—when the person you're calling has not approached you or expressed interest in your products or services.

Of course, everybody hates getting cold calls, but have you ever stopped and wondered why we keep getting cold calls when we all hate them? Here's the dirty little secret: Cold calls work.

Cold calls can be effective, especially if you spend time to find appropriate potential leads. And if your business is stagnant, or you're developing a new product or service line, cold calls can be a relatively inexpensive way to attract new customers.

The most common ways to make cold calls include:

■ Meeting in person

■ Phone calls

■ Direct mail solicitation

■ Mail order catalogs

■ Email

■ Online or mobile sales

What's the secret of cold call success?

■ **Change your perspective.** Most of us think of a sales call as "bothering" the other person. But if you offer something you truly believe meets a real need at a good value, then you're not a bother but a help.

■ **"Qualify" your leads.** We really HATE sales calls when they don't relate to us. Find ways to narrow down your target list. That saves you time and increases your success rate.

■ **Develop a great pitch.** Be clear about what you're offering and the benefits to the customer. Write out your pitch and the most important points well before you make your first call, but don't read it!

■ **Take people literally.** If a prospect says, "I'm not interested right now," believe they mean right NOW. Perhaps they'll be interested another time. Ask if you can call on them at a later time.

■ **Don't be obnoxious.** Take "No" for an answer. If someone's not interested, why waste your time or theirs? Be polite. They may know someone else who's interested or their situation may change.

■ **Mind your manners.** If you walk in on someone and they're on the phone, wait until they're free. If you're phoning, and the person says "Now's not a good time," ask when a good time would be to call back, and get off the phone.

■ **Give yourself a quota.** Set a minimum—but realistic—number of calls you have to make before you can call it quits for the day. Stick to it.

■ **Stay in practice.** Cold calling is difficult, and it's easy to forget how to do it well. So make calls from time to time even when you aren't looking for a lot of new work.

Finally, don't take rejection personally and don't get discouraged. Remember, you've got to kiss a lot of frogs before you find a prince.

58. Create a subscription service

As mentioned, it costs a lot of money to land a customer, so you want to keep customers as long as you can and try to make as much money from each customer that you can. One of the best ways to achieve both those goals is to create a subscription product or service.

A subscription service is one where a customer pays to receive a service or products on a continuing basis. They pay a monthly or annual fee—a fee that continues until the customer cancels it.

The subscription business model is the "holy grail" of business models. You get recurring revenue and an ongoing relationship with customers. You have revenue you can count on. And it takes a conscious action for a customer to STOP paying you, rather than them having to take an action TO pay you. Finally, all of us have had many subscription services—whether to a gym, to a streaming service, to a publication—that we kept paying for long after we had actually stopped using it.

Of course, we've all gotten used to online subscription services—think Netflix—but you can create subscriptions for all kinds of services and many products. There are subscription meal kits, subscription hair color, subscription children's activity boxes, subscription dog treats, and the granddaddy of all time—a "book of the month club." Are there products or services your customers use repeatedly or use up?

Service businesses, too, can look for ongoing revenue streams. Accountants frequently offer bookkeeping or bill-paying services—instead of doing clients' income tax returns once a year, they work for them all year long. What could you offer your customers on a continuing or subscription basis?

59. Sell on social media

Social media platforms have become more than just a place to post announcements of what's going on in your business. You can also use these powerful social networks to actually sell your products or services.

Of course, you can use virtually all the major social media sites to advertise your products or services, to find leads, and to get the word out about your business. Most of these will also allow you to link to your website.

But only a few social media sites allow you to actually sell from their site or to immediately link to a sales opportunity on your site. The two most important are Facebook and Instagram.

To sell on Instagram or Facebook, you'll first need to have a business, not just a personal, presence and you may need to get approval to use some of their more advanced selling tools.

The ways to sell on these sites keep evolving, but at the most simple, you can add "buy buttons." When someone sees a product they want, they can click the "shop" button which takes them to your website where they'll complete the purchase. This saves prospects from hunting all over your website for an item that catches their eye.

If you have products that lend themselves to being sold directly from social media feeds, be sure to search out how you can sell right from these sites. And remember: you can sell gift cards! This would enable you to sell your services or restaurant meals from social media as well as physical products.

60. Enable ecommerce on your website

When the world got shut down due to Covid, customers turned increasingly to shopping online. That behavior is not going to change soon. Customers like the convenience and safety of buying things directly from the web.

But many small businesses don't offer customers the chance to buy from their website—they don't have **ecommerce** capabilities. They may have felt it was too difficult or expensive to set up shop on their website, or they felt they didn't have a product or service that lent itself to being purchased online.

Well, now's the time to rethink that point of view. There are a number of platforms making it incredibly easy—and affordable—for small businesses to add shopping capabilities to their online presence. And by offering gift cards (a service which can be set up with many of these platforms) virtually any b2c (business-to-consumer) product or service can make online sales.

Depending on your needs, you can create a very complicated online store or a very simple one. But if you're not offering customers a chance to buy from your website now, it's time to rethink that!

Here are some of the leading ecommerce platforms particularly aimed at helping small businesses sell online:

- **Shopify.** This all-in-one solution is designed specifically for small business owners who need to set up an ecommerce site, without needing any experience creating websites or wanting to get going quickly. This subscription service helps you manage sales, sales taxes, shipping, inventory, and more. After you create a Shopify account, you can literally start selling in minutes. (www.shopify.com)

- **SquareSpace.** This website builder application enables you to create an entire website, including, if you wish, to make sales from your site. It has a number of ecommerce templates to help you quickly customize your website for your type of products or services. (www.squarespace.com)

■ **Wix.** More limited, but also less expensive, Wix is a good option for creating a very simple ecommerce store. (www.wix.com)

■ **WordPress.** When it comes to creating an ecommerce presence, Wordpress may be more complicated than some of the other options, but you can build a more robust online presence that may meet your specific needs. To make sales, you can use simple PayPal buttons or you can install a robust ecommerce plugin such as WooCommerce, but you'll probably need help. Fortunately, you'll find lots of experienced Wordpress and WooCommerce consultants who can help. (www.wordpress.org)

61. Flirt with crowdfunding

Crowdfunding is not only a novel way to raise money to start a business or to launch a new product, it's also a way for a company to make pre-sales of a product. And your product doesn't have to be brand new—it just has to be novel or attract a particular targeted audience.

As mentioned in the financing section, many people are willing and eager to fund projects that will lead to the launch of innovative consumer products. The backers, or "crowd," provide the money the company needs to produce the products, and in exchange, those backers are the first to get the newfangled item once it becomes available.

As with other forms of funding, you'll have to be prepared—and do your homework. And your business needs to be a good fit for crowdfunding. You'll need to:

■ **Have the right type of business or product.** For crowdfunding success, your idea must be easily understandable by a large number of people (on that platform). Consumer, food, consumer electronics, and fashion products are particularly well suited to this. Complex concepts and many business-to-business ventures are likely to have a harder time gathering widespread support.

■ **Create a compelling video.** A great video helps engage potential funders, as most funders will want to hear your story, see you, and view prototypes of your product (if any).

■ **Raise sufficient funds.** On some crowdfunding platforms, you don't receive any money until your goal amount is raised in total. This means you want to set an achievable fund-raising target. However, on some platforms, you can raise no more than the financial target you originally set. So you want to make sure you are raising enough to execute on your vision. This can be very hard to get right—even for seasoned entrepreneurs.

■ **Choose the right crowdfunding platform.** Make sure the platform you choose meets your particular needs—type of product or service, type of rewards or equity you can give, amount of money you can raise and whether you need to raise the full amount before receiving any of it.

■ **Have good-quality photos as part of your campaign.** Pics help supporters spread the word through social media.

■ **Have a "coolness" factor.** Your idea is more likely to garner support and go viral if it's unique, attractive, or cutting-edge.

■ **Plan a marketing campaign.** You must plan your crowdfunding fundraising campaign like you would for launching any new product. It will take time, effort, and creativity.

A number of platforms enable startups and small businesses to raise funds (and pre-sell their products). The two best known are Kickstarter (www.kickstarter.com) and IndieGoGo (www.indiegogo.com).

WHAT?!

62. Get others to sell for you

You don't have to do everything alone. Working with another company—or companies—can get you more sales in this current environment, you may find it wise to team up with others.

Look for others who can work with you—sell for you—through:

- **Cooperative advertising:** This type of advertising occurs when two companies are mentioned in an advertisement and each company pays part of the costs. If you sell products made by others, ask if they do "co-op" ads. They will usually pay all or much of the cost of the ad. Or create collective ads with a number of small businesses in your neighborhood.

- **Bundling:** In this type of relationship, one company includes another company's product or service as part of a total package. You keep your own identity, but get the advantage of being included in their package.

- **Distribution agreement:** This is an arrangement where one company carries another's product line and sells its products or services to customers. You may find other small businesses that can sell your products or services and take a percentage or you may enter some kind of agreement where you sell each other's products or services.

- **Licensing:** If you or your business has a very well-known and beloved name, think of related businesses that might want to use that name to sell their products or services. For instance, if you have a very popular children's clothing store in your neighborhood, see if a kids' art class program might license your name to sell their online classes, giving you a small percent of each class sold.

- **White Labeling:** Instead of selling your product or service directly, you might license it to another company to sell under its name and brand. This is particularly easy for tech companies and apps to do, but other small manufacturers could look for companies who might want to add your product or service to their own product lineup.

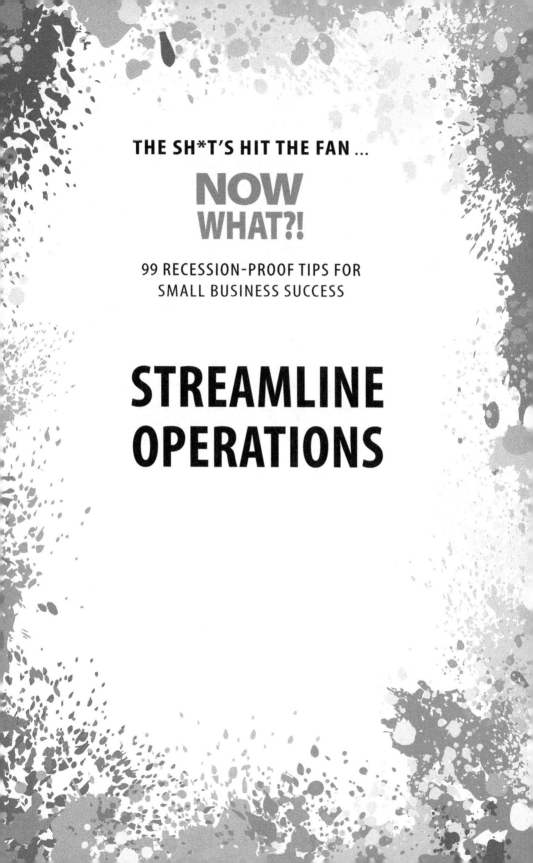

THE SH*T'S HIT THE FAN ...

NOW
WHAT?!

99 RECESSION-PROOF TIPS FOR
SMALL BUSINESS SUCCESS

STREAMLINE
OPERATIONS

What you need to know since the sh*t's hit the fan.

Nothing upended business operations as quickly and as significantly as the response to Covid-19. Virtually every small business in the US had to re-evaluate how it did business. Of course, the first issue was how to stay in business, but right up there was the next question—"How do we actually get the work of our business done in this environment?"

When everything hits the fan, it's time to look at every aspect of the day-to-day aspects of running your business—your operations—to see how to become more efficient, more productive, more careful with all of your resources, including money, time, staff, tangible items. Once again, think and act like a startup—move quickly, try things, make mistakes, learn from them, improve, move on. Assessing and tightening up your operations will not only save you money and reduce headaches now, it will hold you in good stead during bad times and good.

You'll find a lot of tips on how to slim down and streamline your operations in the section, "Start Lean, Stay Lean." In this section, we'll look at some other tips to improve how you run your small business or startup.

63. Work from home

One of the first operational issues you deal with in any business is where you'll work. In this environment, there's a good chance that you're now doing a lot of your work from home. Perhaps you've given up your office space to save money now that you've found that you (and your staff if you have employees) can work productively from home. Perhaps you cannot go back to your workspace safely. Perhaps you're just spending more time in your home office because you have kids at home. Whether you're working part-time or full-time from a home office, it's important to find ways to be as productive as possible in your home office. Be sure to:

■ **Find a good space to work.** If you have a separate room or garage you can turn into an office, that's ideal, especially if you are going to be working from home permanently, for many hours a day, or for an extended period of time. What's important is to carve out a space you can use regularly, and almost exclusively, as your office. If possible, it should be in a place where other family members aren't coming and going during your work hours. Even if you have to use one end of your dining room table, try to have a space without too many distractions. Get a good comfortable office chair, decent lighting, some place for storage for your files, paperwork.

■ **Establish work hours.** One of the most difficult tasks for people who run a business from home is establishing a clear distinction between work life and home life—especially with the constant distractions of emails, texts, and other digital interruptions. It really helps if you establish a work routine that makes you, other workers, your family, and others conscious of when you're working and when you're available. That doesn't mean you have to limit work from 9 am to 5 pm; just establish real working hours. And yes, as part of your regular hours, you can carve time out of your day to spend time with the kids or get some exercise—just let everyone know that's part of the plan.

■ **Find places to meet with customers, team members, or others.** It's likely some work has to be done in person and you'll benefit from some face-to-face interactions to help keep team members motivated and lines of communication clear. Look for spaces where you can have meetings or sales calls. It may be a café, a shared work rent-by-the-hour space, even a park.

■ **Make childcare arrangements, if possible.** It's not realistic to expect to get work done with kids coming in and out, needing help with schoolwork, wanting attention. If possible, consider making childcare arrangements depending on your children's ages and the nature of your work. You may want to seek out other parents who work from home to share or rotate joint child care arrangements. Whatever your arrangement, develop a structured routine for your kids that keeps them busy (and out of your hair) for a set period of time each day so you can get work done.

■ **Deal with pets.** A dog or cat makes working at home less lonely. But just as you can't have a screaming child in the background when you're on a call, you can't have a barking dog—at least not often. If your dog barks a lot and you have to make calls, put it in another room while you work.

STAY SANE!
Use apps to stay productive

It's easy to get distracted when you work at home, and you can quickly find you start spending too much time on social media or on spider solitaire (my downfall!). Fortunately, there are a number of apps to help keep you focused and block out distracting sites and games. Check out apps such as **Freedom** (www.freedom.to) or **Cold Turkey** (www.getcoldturkey.com) or **Self-Control** (www.selfcontrolapp.com).

64. Decide whether you need a separate business address

If you do decide to work from home, for privacy reasons you may not be comfortable using your home address as your business address.

One alternative is to get a Post Office box from the US Postal Service. If you do, however, your address will appear as a "P.O. Box." That may not give the impression you want. Moreover, the Post Office usually doesn't accept mail from private delivery services such as Federal Express or UPS.

An alternative is to rent a mailbox from one of the many private mailbox providers, such as the UPS Store. This gives you the advantage of not giving out your home address, having a secure place to receive mail, and having someone who can sign and receive packages for you.

65. Step up safety

If you have a place of business outside of your home, safety must be an integral part of everything you do, especially in this atmosphere where health has been on everyone's minds.

You want to provide a safe place for yourself, your employees, your customers and anyone else who might come into your place of business. Your employees and customers want to know that you respect them enough to ensure they are safe—or they will stop working for or buying from you.

So, even if you think you do everything safely and cleanly, it's time to step up your efforts:

- Follow all national, state, county, and city rules on all safety matters.

- Ensure your employees understand the importance of keeping everything clean and safe.

- Step up your level of cleanliness and sanitizing. That may mean very frequent sanitizing of surfaces, many more breaks for hand washing.

- Follow the highest level of safety guidelines from respected scientists, experts, and the Center for Disease Control, especially on issues such as social distancing and wearing masks.

- Provide signage informing employees, customers, and visitors what is expected or required of them to ensure everyone's safety.

- Provide signage letting everyone know the steps you are taking to ensure their safety.

- Continually monitor everything to make sure your safety requirements are being implemented and followed by everyone.

Of course, these types of actions cost money. You need to budget funds to ensure such safety procedures, but if people are afraid to be in your place of business, you'll soon be out of business.

66. Go to the cloud

You're almost certainly already using "cloud-based" applications—applications that are hosted, stored, and accessed over the Internet rather than on your own devices. After all, your smart phone is filled with cloud-based apps—whether providing you GPS directions, storing your photos, keeping up with social media posts, and so much more.

And it's possible that you're also using some cloud-based applications for your small business—if for instance, you use gmail, a cloud-based email service. But now's the time to evaluate whether virtually everything you do in your business can be handled in the cloud rather than on your servers, hard drives, or other "terrestrial" devices.

Whatever business need you have, there's almost certainly a cloud-based program that can do the job. You can get cloud-based programs for your document storage, accounting and bookkeeping, your CRM (contact management system), payroll, email, virtual meetings, and so much more. You can even get your basic office functions, such as word processing and spreadsheets, based in the cloud.

There's a reason—actually many reasons—why businesses both large and small have moved so many of their core functions to the cloud, including:

- **Mobility.** You can access your data from anywhere you have Internet access.

- **Low upfront costs.** You can start with only exactly what you need, with little equipment and software costs, and often with the free versions of many apps.

- **Scalability.** You pay only for the number of users or features you need, quickly able to turn those up or down.

- **Safety.** Your data is not stored only on your own devices on your premises, and is often backed up in multiple locations.

■ **Additional computing power.** Online services typically have more capabilities than you—as a small business—could afford to have built and customized for you.

■ **Constantly upgraded.** The app developers continually push upgrades to the service, ensuring you have the latest features without the interruptions of upgrading on-site software.

■ **Predictable costs.** You don't have unexpected outages, the need for IT consultants, and other unpredictable expenses.

Of course, there are also drawbacks to cloud-based applications, including:

■ **Monthly/annual costs.** Unlike software that you purchase once and can use until it gets outdated—often years—you pay a "subscription" fee that adds to your monthly expenses.

■ **Internet-dependent.** For almost all cloud-based applications, you need to be connected to the internet to be able to access the app and/or your data. Some cloud-based services enable you to store a copy of your data on your own device as well, but if your internet connection is weak or unreliable, this can be a big concern.

■ **Security.** Although cloud-based services certainly provide greater security than just storing valuable data on an on-premise server or a laptop, some people fear that their data could be hacked, especially financial data.

STAY SANE!

Control your data

Eventually, employees move on. Make sure YOU are always the administrator/owner of every cloud-based application, so that if an employee who manages your application leaves, you control the application and data, not the departing employee (and they can't hold your data hostage). Whenever an employee leaves, make sure you turn "off" their access to your cloud-based applications immediately (if you are firing or laying them off, turn off their access before you tell them). Make sure you have access to all data of any and every employee—if your top salesperson has been hoarding her customer data in spreadsheets on her computer, you don't want that company asset walking out the door with her if she leaves the company. Set up administrative controls that let you bypass private passwords.

FREE OR ON THE CHEAP

YOU CAN GET A WHOLE RANGE OF CLOUD BASED BUSINESS APPLI-CATIONS—with a basic, fairly large, level of storage—for free or very inexpensively. These suites can include services such as word processing, document storage, spreadsheets, presentation, contact management, and more. Check out **Google Docs** (www.docs.google.com), **Zoho** (www.zoho.com), **Office 365** (www.office.com).

67. Outsource everything you can

In the section "Start Lean, Stay Lean," we've talked about "just-in-time" inventory, but one way to stay lean in your business and to keep overhead low is to have "just-in-time" everything: staff, business services, equipment, vehicles, delivery, whatever. If you can just hire what you need, when you need it, for only as long as you need it, you'll keep money in your bank account.

The way to do that is to outsource as many aspects of your business to others as you can. Of course, you may pay more for each hour, each service, or each product than if you had in-house staff, your own manufacturing, or equipment and vehicles you own, but you have much more flexibility and far less initial outlay. In fact, you can grow a fairly big—and profitable—company by letting others do most of the work for you.

In an economically challenging environment—especially where you are trying new things—outsourcing can be a way to introduce a new product or service without having to invest in the infrastructure of creating that product or service in-house.

For examples, many companies outsource the manufacturing of their products, outsource their technical support services, outsource the sales and distribution of their products, or just outsource their janitorial services. You can outsource to companies in your own country or look for international suppliers.

Many suppliers offer their products in a **white label** form—enabling you to put your brand on products they make, so your customers never know that you weren't the maker.

Outsourcing offers many benefits:

■ **It saves money.** By hiring another business that specializes in a certain aspect of operations—say, manufacturing, order fulfillment, or even customer service—you reduce the size of your permanent staff and drive your fixed costs down.

■ **It frees you up to focus.** By contracting out non-core functions, you can concentrate on the aspects about your business that matter the most, rather than those that are peripheral. For instance, a company may keep all the design functions of a new electronic device in-house but outsource manufacturing. After all, you want to maintain control over those elements of your business that give you a competitive advantage.

■ **Others might do a better job than you.** Another company might do the work more proficiently and efficiently than you can. For example, a new company may not be proficient in human resource and benefits issues and use outsourced HR consultants, who stay up-to-date on changing labor laws and practices.

■ **You may get to market faster.** A contract manufacturer likely already has the equipment, processes, and staff in place to produce your product. Acquiring all those yourself would take far longer, meaning a much longer time before you could begin to make sales—and bring in money.

Perhaps you'll outsource yourself or your business, serving as an outside provider or as an independent contractor for other companies that hire you on an as-needed basis. This could open up a whole new market for you!

68. Diversify your supply chain

Many businesses have goods or materials coming into the company and finished products or services going out—whether it is raw materials to make your products, food to make your restaurant's offerings, inventory to sell in your retail store. The companies you rely on to provide you with incoming goods are essential to the continuing operation of your business. They constitute your "supply chain," and how you manage that chain is called supply chain management.

In the current environment, it's likely that you are going to experience some difficulties and delays with your suppliers at some point. They may be short of stock, have lengthy delivery times, or get out of the business altogether. Try not to be dependent on just one supplier; your financial future will be too vulnerable if it fails you. Work to develop excellent relationships with your suppliers; you'll want them to feel that you are in a partnership together so that they will try to do everything possible to meet your needs. Be responsive to their needs, as well; work out payment plans and communication methods to reduce pressures on them.

69. Remember customer service

Remember, your work isn't finished when you produce a product or secure an order from a customer. You still need to make sure your customer receives the product ordered, in good condition, and in a timely fashion. You need to know that you've satisfied your customer.

In response to all the changes in the economy and society, you'll almost certainly be experimenting with new ways to make money—new products, services, and/or locations. That means you'll do many things wrong, and so will your employees if you have employees. Try to learn from your mistakes. You'll need to keep customers' expectations realistic, and say you're sorry and try to make things right when something goes wrong, be patient with your employees, and seek feedback.

Build sufficient flexibility into your policies so that you can easily handle unusual or difficult requests. Train all employees—from the shipping clerk to the sales representative—in customer service and empower employees to make certain decisions on the spot (such as accepting returns) instead of requiring each customer request to be approved by a manager. Make it easy for your customers to give you feedback, so you can learn what's working and what's not.

70. Disaster-proof your business

As we've all learned, the unexpected happens. Bad things happen even to good companies. Many businesses were shut down—or had their operations seriously cut back—due to Covid-19. But an emergency could be a natural disaster—flood, fire, earthquake—or something more mundane such as a burglary, a power outage, a pipe breaking. In addition to natural disasters, emergencies also come in the form of illnesses and accidents.

Look at those things that are absolutely critical for you to do business, and find ways to make certain they're able to continue even after an emergency, the loss of a critical supplier, the absence of a key employee.

As with many aspects of running a business, you need to plan ahead. Do the following now, so you'll be prepared for the next emergency.

- **Cross train.** At least two people should know how to do each job—pay bills, run payroll, answer phones, fulfill orders, and so on.

- **Develop an operations manual.** Ask each employee to type up in detail the steps for each task and to take any necessary screen shots. Print this information and place it in a binder where someone filling in can easily find it.

- **Protect passwords.** For all of your technology, online accounts, banking, and so forth, keep a spare up-to-date list of passwords in a lawyer's or trusted family member's safe in case something happens to you or your place of business.

- **Make it accessible.** Someone extremely trustworthy should have a copy of the key to your building, office, or safe.

- **Examine your insurance.** In addition to insurance to cover loss of physical equipment, records, and inventory, you might want business interruption insurance.

71. Protect your data

One of the biggest problems small businesses have after a disaster in terms of getting loans or insurance is not having access to their records, especially their financial records. Make sure you develop procedures to safeguard your records and data.

The best way to store your data is in the cloud. In that way, you'll have access to your data wherever you have internet access even if you no longer have access to your premises or your computers are unavailable. Get in the habit of using cloud-based data storage systems continually.

Yes, many small business owners are reluctant to keep financial information on cloud-based applications. Other small business owners may be reluctant to change their habits of just keeping their data on on-premise storage or their laptops. But if something happens, without your data, you will have a very hard time getting your company back up and running, and an even harder time collecting on insurance or any government assistance. So do not store your data—especially your financial information—on your premises only, where it can be damaged in a disaster or stolen, or on a laptop, which you could lose.

FREE OR ON THE CHEAP

ONLINE DATA STORAGE. Upload your most important documents, photos, videos and more to the cloud. Some apps provide a level of storage free. Once you reach the storage limits of the free versions these apps offer, you simply upgrade to the next level.

■ **Dropbox** (www.dropbox.com)

■ **Box** (www.box.com)

■ **Google Drive** (drive.google.com)

■ **Apple icloud** (www.icloud.com)

---

72. "Green" your operations

The fact is that every company can save money—and help the planet at the same time—by taking a few easy steps to reduce waste.

- **Shipping.** Your green efforts don't have to end when the production process does. Do you use the most efficient methods to ship? Can you cut down on your product's packaging? Can you reduce the weight of your product or shipping materials? If so, you'll save money on shipping and use less energy.

- **Water.** If you use water as part of your manufacturing process, find ways to use less, or recycle it to water your landscaping.

- **Energy.** For many companies, energy consumption is a large expense. Put heating and cooling on timers, control when machinery and equipment comes on and off in your manufacturing plant, choose energy efficient equipment. Your printers, monitors, and copiers are all on "standby" mode, meaning they still consume a bit of energy—so unplug those each night or put those on timers as well.

- **Supplies and materials.** Use recycled and reclaimed materials if possible and buy supplies that arrive with less packaging. Encourage employees to use less paper and recycle what they do use.

THE SH*T'S HIT THE FAN ...

NOW
WHAT?!

99 RECESSION-PROOF TIPS FOR
SMALL BUSINESS SUCCESS

MOTIVATE
AND
MANAGE
YOUR TEAM

What you need to know since the sh*t's hit the fan.

In a time of great economic or social change, the person in charge of an organization makes all the difference between success and failure, between stability and chaos. Keep in mind that during these times of change, your team members may be worried and easily distracted. They are concerned about their futures, their financial well-being, the health and security of their families. You—as the leader of their team—have to provide even more leadership, more confidence and stability, than in good times. Your attitude toward your business and your employees shapes their attitude toward you and their jobs.

It's also likely that you'll be making a lot of changes in your business to respond to current conditions; you'll be pivoting to stay more resilient. Those changes, too, will make employees and team members anxious. So it's more important than ever for you to think carefully about how you manage and motivate your team, how you communicate with them, what you share with them.

If you want your business to grow, to survive and thrive regardless of the economy, you need extra brains—not just extra brawn—no matter how smart you are personally. Those who are on the front lines of carrying out a task—whether it be making a product, making a sale, or shipping the boxes—are usually in the best position to suggest improvements. You need employees who can think and who can act—and you need to be the kind of manager and motivator who can make that happen.

73. Motivate yourself

Before you can motivate others, you'll need to find ways to motivate yourself. You may not think that's a challenge, but in difficult economic times, in times when you're making many changes—some of which will inevitably not work out the way you'd hoped—it's easy to get discouraged and exhausted. But remember, the most important member of your team is YOU.

You are the spark plug for your own business. Your entire team looks to you, takes their cues from you. If you are discouraged, unmotivated, pessimistic—your team will be too. If you are positive, motivated, optimistic—your team will be too. You need to be able to continually ignite the energy, the passion, the purpose of your entire team. When the sparks don't seem to ignite, you've got to do something about it.

When you find your motivation and energy flagging, here are some steps to take:

- **Remind yourself of your long-term goals.** Look at the business you're building not just the tasks you're doing. Remember why you wanted to be your own boss, to build a business.

- **Develop a plan of action.** Examining what you want to do and what kind of steps you'll need to take to accomplish those steps can help you feel focused and keep yourself motivated.

- **Make a list.** If you don't have the desire to develop a plan, at least make a "To Do" list. Having tasks assigned each day gives you a structure for getting back to work.

- **Make some appointments.** Go on, get out there. Meeting, virtually or in-person, with others—whether customers, prospects, or even vendors— gets you talking about your business (hopefully enthusiastically) again.

- **Talk to another business owner.** Often, talking to another business owner—especially one who is also working thoughtfully to survive and succeed—can help give you both ideas and support. But avoid those pessimistic owners who are not as willing as you to make the changes necessary to survive.

■ **Get enough sleep, exercise, and eat well.** Taking care of yourself helps you to have the energy and stamina to face what you need to do and helps keep your mental state stable.

■ **Rearrange your workspace.** If you're unmotivated, do something visual to help change your mental attitude.

■ **Read motivational quotes.** They may seem cheesy, but sometimes a motivational quote can actually motivate you.

FREE OR ON THE CHEAP

PRODUCTIVITY APPS. Search for "productivity apps" and about 200,000,000 results pop up. We've narrowed that down a bit for you. The following apps will help you get your work done in less time:

■ RESCUETIME. Offers tools to track how your use your time online and courses for how to use that time more productively. (www.rescuetime.com)

■ COLD TURKEY. Block the websites, apps, and games you find most distracting on your computer so you can get work done. (https://getcoldturkey.com)

■ EVERNOTE. Store your research, find your images and documents quickly, and capture those great half-dozen new business ideas you have before breakfast. Spend your time working, not searching. (https://evernote.com)

■ ANY.DO. Create to-do lists that sync across all your devices. Connect your calendar, set reminders, share lists, and more. (www.any.do)

■ NOTION. Take notes, create company wikis, and manage tasks, all in one app. (www.notion.so)

---

74. Manage a remote team

Some of your team may be working from home. Some may be working from the office. Some may be working from another state. Fortunately, technology makes it possible to run your business and stay connected with your team when you're not all working in the same physical location. As with most aspects of business, a little bit of planning pays off. Set up regular team virtual staff meetings. Learn how to use that project management software you signed up for ages ago. Make sure you organize important company files in such a way that your employees can easily and quickly find the information they need to do their jobs.

Here's how to improve the productivity of a remote and/or scattered team:

■ **Communicate via chat.** Need a quick answer? Want to ask how everyone's weekend went? Send it through chat, not email, and keep your Inbox unclogged. There are many online chat tools—as well as just plain text messaging—that can be quicker (and some, more organized) ways to communicate.

■ **Set up a group calendar.** Keep track of upcoming events, vacations, deadlines, and meetings at a glance. The simplest way to do this is through Google, Apple, or Outlook calendars.

■ **Structure the workweek.** Schedule daily check ins and weekly (at least) virtual staff meetings, taking differing time zones into account. In addition to business, include casual conversations in these meetings. Ask employees how they're doing.

■ **Manage your team.** You don't want to micromanage employees but you do want to set clear expectations so everyone knows what their responsibilities are—and what yours are as the boss.

■ **Help your employees set up a workspace at home.** Give employees advice on how to create a productive workspace wherever they are. Consider paying for their WiFi, or at least a portion of it. And if they have childcare responsibilities at home, discuss with them how they can balance that with their realistic job responsibilities.

■ **Turn it off.** No one wants you bombarding them with your late-night texts. Turn off your tech at the end of the day and encourage your employees to do the same—otherwise you'll all find yourselves burning out.

FREE OR ON THE CHEAP

SLACK, an online communication tool, includes chat among its many, many features (www.slack.com). Slack has taken the world by storm as it is such a useful way to manage company or project communication. You can also use an app such as Skype, Whatsapp, iMessages, and so on, for instant messaging. Slack has a free offering for very small businesses.

---

75. Master virtual meetings

Video meetings are now the norm in many businesses, especially when it comes to professional and B2B (business-to-business) companies. But even if you're in a business where you wouldn't expect to hold virtual meetings with your own team—such as construction—you may find that some customers, vendors, or collaborators now want to meet virtually rather than in person.

Fortunately, video conferencing has proven to be an effective way to do business, and most everyone is now comfortable with holding video meetings—often just referred to as "Zooming" (because of the popular Zoom video application).

We've found we really like our Zoom meetings—they've turned out to be more productive and enjoyable that in-person meetings! So it's time to step up your game and learn to do video conferencing effectively:

- **Learn the technology.** Online video conferencing tools are now remarkably easy. In fact, they're so easy to get up and running that you may overlook some of the tools available in them. Besides learning how to share screens, check out functions like chat and breakout rooms to enable more interaction among those participating in a virtual meeting.

- **Check time zones.** Before you set the time for a meeting, keep in mind the time zones of participants if you have participants in vastly different time zones.

- **Schedule meetings.** Just like in-person meetings, set dates and times in advance for these virtual meetings, so everyone knows they're "real" business meetings.

- **Use video.** Some people don't like having their cameras turned on—and if it's a client or prospect, you'll have to abide by their wishes. But there's more engagement when participants turn on their video. Not only do people like looking at faces, it keeps your staff from doing other things at the same time.

■ **Involve many people.** Sure, you have a lot to say, but use virtual meetings to get everyone involved, getting their ideas, their feedback, their buy-in.

■ **Reduce distractions.** Make sure you've got your pets and kids out of the room—and ask participants to do the same. Have them "mute" if there's noise in the background.

■ **Have an agenda.** In small businesses, an agenda doesn't have to be very formal, but you'll be more productive if you have a list of things you want to discuss and accomplish.

■ **Include some personal chit chat.** These virtual meetings are also important in building a sense of team and keeping remote workers motivated. Spend some time at the beginning of the virtual meeting checking in to see how everyone is and what's going on with them.

■ **End with action items.** People are more likely to be engaged in future virtual meetings if they know that something specific comes out of them. Have assignments, deadlines, actions to take.

■ **Pay a little bit.** While most virtual meeting services have a free version, you may want to step up to a paid version to get a bit more flexibility and features.

One other note—don't forget phone calls! While texts and emails are both useful communication methods, it's often easier—and your intent is clearer—with a phone call. It's far easier for a text to be misunderstood than a phone call.

FREE OR ON THE CHEAP

There are a number of ways for you to engage with your team, customers, and prospects virtually. Just a few:

- **Zoom** (www.zoom.com)

- **Skype** (www.skype.com)

- **Google Meet, formerly Hangouts** (https://apps.google.com/meet/)

- **WebEx** (www.webex.com)

- **Facebook Messenger Rooms**

- **MicrosoftTeams** (https://www.microsoft.com/en-us/microsoft-365/microsoft-teams/group-chat-software)

You can also add a number of people to "Facetime" calls if they are all on Apple devices. For free phone conference calls, check out **FreeConference Call** (www.freeconferencecall.com).

76. Use "just-in-time" people

Remember—you are going to "start lean, stay lean" in your business, and that means keeping your staff as lean as possible too. Just as you've learned to try to keep overhead down with "just-in-time" inventory, you can keep your personnel costs down with just-in-time people. What do we mean by that?

Recognize that there are some jobs that need permanent full-time or part-time workers and some people you want to keep attached to your team by making them permanent. But other tasks can be outsourced to independent contractors or can use workers on a seasonal rather than permanent basis.

- **Independent contractors.** Most companies use outside providers to perform certain tasks. You can outsource all kinds of responsibilities, including bookkeeping, website design and hosting, payroll management, public relations, marketing, employee training, and even many aspects of production. To provide these functions, you can either hire self-employed individuals—independent contractors—or use outside companies. And just because they're independent doesn't mean that they're not important, ongoing members of your team. Include appropriate ones in your planning, regular staff meetings, team get-togethers, etc.

- **Temporary employees.** Many companies are seasonal, and you may only need employees during your busy times. You can hire full- or part-time employees on a temporary basis. If you find excellent workers, see if there are ways to stay connected with them during your off-season—either through finding work for them to do or at least communicating with them and keeping them involved in some company activities. That way, they'll be more likely to come back to you when you need them.

FREE OR ON THE CHEAP

FIND YOUR TEAM. These apps help you find and recruit employees and hire independent contractors. On some, you'll find thousands of contractors for projects such as software and app development, website design, writing, marketing, and so on. On others, you can post your job openings.

■ **Upwork** (www.upwork.com)

■ **PeoplePerHour** (www.peopleperhour.com)

■ **Guru** (www.guru.com)

■ **Indeed Employer** (www.indeed.com)

■ **Linkedin Recruiter** (https://business.linkedin.com/talent-solutions/post-jobs)

NOW WHAT?!

77. Communicate often and effectively

In uncertain times—and times of change—communication with your team members is more important than ever. Your employees want to know what is expected of them—especially as roles and responsibilities may evolve or change—they want to feel secure, and they want to feel appreciated. It's your job as a manager and leader to communicate with each and every one of them to accomplish those ends.

And in times of change, you want to hear from your employees and team members. You need their input, good ideas, and feedback to be able to respond quickly to changing conditions, especially opportunities that your employees may notice that you might miss.

Ensure that you're communicating often and well with your team—and that they're communicating with you. Effective communication—whether you are in charge of a team of 100 or a single employee—by definition involves a two-way conversation. Information must flow as easily from your employees to you as it does from you to them. Effective communication with your team members (not just employees but critical contractors) is always a major part of your role as company leader, but it is particularly important during difficult economic times.

78. Share relevant information

It's tough as a manager to know how transparent you want to be with your team, especially when your finances may be uncertain. On the one hand, you want them to know everything relevant for them to do their jobs well—that means sharing quite a lot. For instance, that might mean letting your employees know that a big client is unhappy, so they can pay more attention to that client's work and satisfaction. On the other hand, you want employees to feel secure, and letting them know that a big client is in jeopardy may only make them fearful. Holding back too much information means employees might overhear you talking, hear rumors from others, or otherwise sense that something is wrong, and may be more fearful than if you shared important information in a positive way.

Share all the information that employees need to both do their jobs and to help you devise new ways to address and solve problems that arise in your business. But try—as much as you can—to do it with an air of positivity, so that employees are not constantly worried about their job security.

NOW
WHAT?!

79. Provide clear direction

Being clear about responsibilities and expectations can be tough, especially in a time of great change in your business. You may not always be exactly clear about what needs to be done yourself. But try as hard as you can to think through what you need done before you give employees tasks.

When something is big or new, don't just hand off assignments. Try to explain *why* something needs to be done, not just *what* needs to be done. You have to spend time communicating the specific goals, tasks, the customer or competitive pressures involved, deadlines, and even budgets. The more your employees get a complete view of their work, the more likely they are to help you come up with innovative and cost-cutting solutions, and the more understanding they'll be if a project suddenly comes under a time crunch and requires overtime, or if budgets are suddenly tight due to cost overruns.

FREE OR ON THE CHEAP

PROJECT MANAGEMENT APPS. Use these apps to stay on top of projects and get things done with your team, making it easier to track specific assignments and progress.

- **Asana** (https://asana.com)

- **Wrike** (www.wrike.com)

- **Teamwork** (www.teamwork.com)

- **Taskade** (www.taskade.com)

- **Trello** (https://trello.com)

---

80. Offer timely and constructive feedback

Absolutely no one likes to get criticized. And as the old saying goes, "No one ever nagged a dog into doing what you want." Criticizing, nagging, harping—all those are ways to make employees LESS productive rather than more productive.

When something goes wrong—and something always does go wrong—try to find ways to communicate that are constructive: sticking to specific actions that could have been taken to avoid the problem. Ask the employee, "What could you do differently next time?" instead of just blaming them for the problem.

Rather than thinking of it as criticism—which could slant what you say in a negative direction—consider it as encouragement to improve. Employees thrive when you stress what they've done well and make suggestions on how they could do even better.

Some people thrive under pressure; most don't. In this environment, your staff is dealing with many changes. Most will take time to get up to speed. The best way to reduce the learning curve and accelerate productivity is to understand this and make the employees feel safe in a blame-free environment. This means understanding when someone makes mistakes, even fails outright, and trying to treat such events as positive learning experiences.

NOW WHAT?!

81. Share goals and a sense of purpose

Employees are highly motivated when they, like you, feel their work is accomplishing something important. Even the seemingly most mundane business usually has an important purpose; after all, you're meeting a customer need or desire. For example, you may be running a diaper service—a dirty business indeed. But what you're really doing is providing an important service for new parents at a time when they're the most hassled and concerned about their baby's well-being. Helping your employees to understand the social and personal value in their work makes them more satisfied on a day-to-day basis.

82. Give employees authority as well as responsibility

Delegating responsibility to employees is a good first step. But it only takes you halfway to your goal of being a good boss.

For employees to be effective, productive, and motivated, they need **authority** as well as **responsibility**. This means you have to learn to be comfortable with people making some decisions that are different from those you'd make and recognizing some decisions are just different—not wrong.

Imagine you own a café. You know your repeat business and online reviews depend on how your servers treat customers, so you continually remind your servers about the importance of treating customers well, you base their raises on how customers rate them, and you tell them repeatedly that you trust them to ensure that customers never leave the restaurant unhappy. But unless you also give them the authority to do such things as offer a free dessert because of the long wait for a table, you are more liable to frustrate your employees than empower them.

Sometimes, however, employees will indeed make what turns out to be a wrong decision—or at least a decision you wouldn't want to make. How do good bosses handle that? They spend time with the employee listening, learning why a decision was made, and then discussing how they could have made a better choice, rather than rehashing the history and looking for blame.

When managers trust and empower employees to think about how to solve problems—not merely to carry out specific tasks as specifically instructed—they give those employees the potential to unleash impressive amounts of creativity and energy. And, not incidentally, you'll retain the people you've spent a lot of time and money hiring.

83. Recognize effort and accomplishment

Everyone wants to have their hard work acknowledged, and people thrive when they feel appreciated. A simple "thank you" can make your staff members feel that they're a valuable, contributing part of your team. Look for opportunities to recognize both effort and achievement by members of your team. Recognition has been shown to be an extremely positive motivator of employee behavior.

- **Rewards reinforce behavior.** Even small rewards—whether cash, promotions, time off, gifts, or something as simple as a candy bar or certificate of achievement—show that you appreciate what they are doing for you and your business and keep employees wanting to do more.

- **Recognition keeps people motivated.** Studies have shown that recognition without rewards is more powerful then rewards without recognition. And research has also proven that intermittent positive feedback is the best possible way to motivate people to do better. In other words, getting frequent but not necessarily predictable praise in response to good job performance is a time-honored way to get more out of your employees. Conversely, intermittent negative feedback is among the worst behaviors you can engage in, as it fosters insecurity and fear among workers.

- **Celebrate with your employees.** Help them feel like they are part of a team, working together toward a common goal. The most successful companies create a sense of partnership and teamwork. One of the best ways to do that is to celebrate successes. Don't just wait for big successes. Taking your staff to lunch to celebrate when a big project is completed makes everyone feel a sense of accomplishment and belonging.

84. Consider hiring during a downturn

As a result of changes in the economy, your business may be changing or growing, and you may need new people on your team to make that happen. You may find yourself needing new skills—a digital marketer instead of an outside salesperson, a delivery driver instead of someone in the warehouse. Now—surprisingly—may be the best time to hire and get the help you need to survive and thrive.

It's not fun to say this, but high unemployment means there are lots of great job prospects for your small business or startup. This means that some of the most skilled workers are available to help you take your business to the next level. And although it's awful when recent college graduates can't find good jobs, that means there are lots of eager, smart, young people you can add to your team.

Times of high unemployment offer employers:

- ■ **Cheaper labor.** Prospects recognize they may have to take lower wages or salaries to get a good job.

- ■ **Talented employees.** In good times, it's often hard for small companies to compete against big corporations for the best people. In bad times, even highly talented, experienced employees are willing to work for small companies.

- ■ **Flexible workers.** Job prospects are more willing to work around your needs and schedule, including being more open to part-time work or off-hours, working from home or working on premises.

- ■ **Greater choice of independent contractors.** Just as more job prospects are available, in down economic times you're more likely to find a large pool of talented people willing to work as independent contractors.

- ■ **Experienced retirees.** Recessionary conditions mean many workers accepted early retirement packages. This means many more experienced workers looking for part-time or full-time roles to use the skills they've gained over a lifetime.

So if you need extra talent to help you successfully navigate the changes in the economy, now is the time to consider hiring.

85. Hire for attitude, train for skills

In a small business or startup, every single member of your team—whether an employee or independent contractor—counts. One underperforming team member, one person with a negative or pessimistic attitude, one person who gossips or creates tension—is like a virus infecting your whole operation.

The first job you have when building a great team is to hire well—look for terrific talent, with not only the right experience but, more importantly, the right attitude.

When advertising for a job, the emphasis is usually on the specific skill set you need—knowledge of computer programs, experience with sales, or the like. And, of course, that's what you first look for—and is easiest to screen applicants for.

But once someone starts the job, their attitude toward work, their enthusiasm for the job, and their willingness to take responsibility makes a major difference in whether they are a great contributor or someone who just plods along.

Of course, you need certain skills for some jobs—you're not going to teach someone complex computer programming skills, for example—but when deciding between two fairly equal candidates (especially if the specific skills can be taught easily), your decision should favor the candidate who appears to have the best work attitude.

As you look for new team members, search for indications of a good, positive attitude, not just the specific skill set you need.

NOW WHAT?!

86. Hire diverse candidates

As a small business owner, you need all the talent, energy, enthusiasm, and smarts you can get. And you need different ideas and points of view, especially in times of economic and social change, to help you more effectively and successfully pivot and take advantage of opportunities.

But all too often, people tend to hire people who are similar to themselves. After all, our comfort level is naturally higher with those who resemble ourselves. But that means we are often missing the best candidates for a job, or finding those who can help us expand our team to better serve both our current and potential customers or find a fresh approach that can bring us success.

Here's a story of how diversity can lead to success. The snack food "Flamin' Hot Cheetos" was created by an 18-year-old Hispanic janitor at the PepsiCo plant that made Cheetos—in large part because the CEO had asked every employee (including janitors) to "take ownership" of the company. It's now one of the snack food brand's biggest sellers.

The best businesses use the talents of diverse people with diverse personalities. They bring fresh ideas and perspectives that may differ from yours, all of which may help you reach other types of customers as well.

But how do you go about hiring more diverse candidates in your small business? One way is through blind hiring. A name often reveals gender and sometimes race. An address or college name could also indicate race or socio-economic status. Graduation dates give a strong clue as to age. Given this kind of demographic information, even the most socially conscious small business owners may pass over an amazing candidate due to pre-conceived notions that are so ingrained in our society, they likely don't even realize they have them.

One thing you can do is to simply ask candidates to eliminate this information from their resumes before they submit them. You'll have their contact information, which generally reveals very little information about your candidate. Once you have narrowed down your candidates—and before learning their identities—you then can set up interviews with the most promising ones.

If you tend to hire people that look like you—your gender, race, alma mater, and age—blind hiring can help you assemble a more diverse team.

NOW WHAT?!

87. Sharpen everyone's skills

The world is changing, and so must you. To survive, stay competitive, foster new ideas, energize your business, and keep your employees and yourself engaged, you need to be constantly learning and sharpening the team's skills.

There are lots of ways to improve your skill set and knowledge base. Industry associations typically have online courses, conferences (some may be virtual), webinars, and just plain group chats to share emerging ideas, tools, technologies related to your industry.

The same is true with community entrepreneurship programs. There are many local business groups—from local chambers of commerce, Small Business Development Centers, women or ethnic business groups, meetup groups, and more. They typically have educational programs.

Community colleges are a terrific source of training—often offering courses aimed at specific skills or industries. Many of these courses are offered online or in the evenings or weekends to accommodate working people.

And then there's a whole slew of online learning platforms. The biggest problem with the current plethora of online courses is deciding which ones to take! You'll find virtual training on management, business writing, finance, marketing, coding, language, graphic design, website development, and more. Platforms to check out:

- **edX.** Find courses from top US schools, including Stanford, Harvard, and MIT. Many are free. (www.edx.org)

- **Udemy.** Sign up your entire team for a course or take different courses individually. (www.udemy.com)

- **Coursera.** Learn from top schools and businesses alike. (www.coursera.com)

- **LinkedIn Learning.** Subscribe and get access to the entire library of online classes. (www.linkedin.com/learning)

RECESSION-
PROOF
YOUR
BUSINESS

What you need to know since the sh*t's hit the fan.

It doesn't take a global pandemic to cause a recession—recessions happen fairly regularly. The reality is that sooner or later, virtually every long-standing business will face having to deal with changing external economic conditions. Whether you're just launching your business or working to ensure the sustainability of your existing business, it's smart to see if you can build in strategies to make your company less vulnerable to the fluctuating highs and lows of the economy. And many businesses are seasonal businesses—highly dependent on a make-or-break limited time of year for their survival. If yours is such a business, look for ways to smooth out your income so your business can weather a bad season or two.

88. Choose a niche—or a few niches

It's often far easier for a small or startup company to attract customers by focusing on a specific market segment—or niche—rather than trying to win every customer imaginable. Choosing a niche means focusing on something that your customers immediately recognize as serving them—making you stand out from your competitors.

As you try new things to survive and thrive in a recessionary market, a good way to experiment is to target different niche markets. In many cases, this will require little or no change to your actual products or services, just focusing your marketing efforts on the specific group, perhaps only changing some of your language and images on some web pages to highlight that you serve a particular market.

Keep in mind that the word niche doesn't necessarily define the market as small, but rather, as specialized and identifiable. A niche is immediately understandable:

- Hair care products for women with curly hair

- Bedding for people with allergies

- Accounting services specializing in serving dental practices

- Publisher specializing in entrepreneurship and business planning (that's PlanningShop!)

An important thing to note about a niche is that it must be based on objective factors. When asked what makes their business unique, most entrepreneurs will say something like, "We give exceptional customer service," or "We do the best job." Those are subjective criteria. A niche—or subset of an overall market—can be identified easily by objective factors such as demographics, industry, activities engaged in, life stage, and so on.

Targeting a specific niche makes your marketing efforts more effective—and often less expensive. Through search engines and social media sites, for example, you can very narrowly target your advertising. For instance, if you had a retail store selling outdoor recreation equipment—a relatively broad category, it would be expensive and difficult to advertise against larger outdoor outfitters. Instead, if you specifically targeted Facebook users in your geographic area who are senior citizens who like to kayak, it would be less expensive and more effective to buy search terms such as "kayaks for seniors" limited to your specific zip codes.

Specializing may also enable you to charge more for your products and services. That's because many customers will readily pay more for goods specially tailored for them, especially if those products or services are hard to find. You might, for instance, be able to charge more if you are a marketing consultant specializing in digital marketing for gyms than if you just identify yourself as a "marketing consultant." Niche products and services also often generate powerful word-of-mouth activity.

Keep in mind that you can target more than one niche, especially if your products or services require little or no customization for a niche. For example, an accounting firm that specializes in doing accounting work for dentists could also have another webpage indicating they have a specialty in serving optometrists and another one for small business customers.

89. Look for counter-cyclical lines of business

No industry is "recession-proof," but some industries do better in down economies than others. And no individual business operates in a vacuum; the forces that affect your industry as a whole will inevitably affect your business as well.

The economy goes in cycles—sometimes up, sometimes down. So it's good to consider what industry you are in and what steps you can take to mitigate the effect of economic cycles—particularly recessions and down economies—on your specific business.

Of course, if you already have an existing business, you are already in a specific industry, and it may be difficult (and expensive) to change. But if you're just starting your business, or you are at a critical inflection point in your business, you'd be wise to consider whether you can choose—or pivot to—an industry that is less vulnerable to economic downturns.

Of course, Covid-19 presented a unique set of circumstances—with almost the entire economy shutting down at once. And consumer and business behavior was less predictable in the midst and aftermath of a pandemic than in normal economic cycles. Nevertheless, you'd do well to look at which industries are more resilient than others.

Traditionally, some industries, such as groceries, personal care products, pharmaceuticals, alcoholic drinks, and low-cost entertainment, are fairly immune to economic cycles. People buy shampoo whether the economy is booming or busting (though they may buy less expensive shampoo in bad times).

Most industries do better when the economy does better: industries such as construction, large consumer items (autos, furniture), hospitality, and tourism all prosper when the economy is healthy and typically suffer when the economy is weak. Industries dependent on new business formation or business expansion, such as commercial real estate, office and technical furniture and equipment also do better in strong economies than when businesses are contracting.

Some industries are ***counter-cyclical,*** doing relatively better in poor economies than strong ones: industries such as discount stores, used car dealers, and any kind of industry that caters to repairing, rather than replacing, high ticket items, such as auto repair.

Ideally, see if you can find ways you can build in aspects of your business that can do well both in good times and in bad—such as having both discount and premium lines of business. See how you can expand to offer different lines of business: some that serve customers who are flush, and some that serve customers who are struggling.

NOW WHAT?!

90. Look to others in your industry

Small business owners are independent. Startups like to think they're disruptive. But the reality is that no business operates totally outside of its own industry. Others in your industry are facing, or have faced, the same—or similar—problems as you. And believe it or not, some other small businesses and startups in your industry have come up with innovative approaches to solving some of those problems.

Sharing information with others in your industry—learning from others like you, perhaps in different locations—can help you ride out the ups and downs of economic, social, and market conditions.

How can you learn from others in your industry?

- **Check out industry associations.** Whatever industry you're in, there's an association—or a number of associations—serving that industry. According to the IRS, there were 66,985 industry associations in 2013 (the last year for which there's data). ASAE, the main membership group for associations, has over 45,000 members. That's a lot of associations. Some places to look to find an association right for you:

  PlanningShop's directory of trade associations https://planningshop.com/associations/

  Directory of Associations www.directoryofassociations.com

  Rutgers University directory of associations https://libguides.rutgers.edu/c.php?g=336557&p=2266143

- **Look for LinkedIn or other social media groups for your industry or concerns.** LinkedIn users have created all kinds of industry-related groups. Following some of their posts—and adding questions or concerns of your own—may help you find counter-cyclical actions appropriate for your business.

- **Ask others in your industry that you know.** Word-of-mouth is always a good way to start. Don't just ask for their solutions, ask for the resources and sources they use to find solutions.

NOW WHAT?!

91. Reduce your dependence on one season

A remarkable number of small businesses are seasonal businesses. The most obvious, of course, are businesses in season-dependent tourist destinations—such as ski resorts, beach communities, winter getaway locales. But even those far away from the beach or the ski slopes can be impacted by the ebb and flow of seasonal cash flow. For example, many retail businesses live or die based on how they do during the crucial Thanksgiving-Christmas holiday season.

Being a seasonal business makes your business more vulnerable, not just in recessions, but when unexpected outside occurrences (such as Covid, national emergencies, natural disasters such as fires or floods) upset normal seasonal buying patterns.

It's wise to consider ways to reduce your dependence on one season to make your company more financially robust year-round. Some ways to do that:

- **Develop counter-seasonal lines.** Diversify your offerings to transform your company into a year-round business. For instance, many lawn care businesses in cold climates offer snow removal services in winter. If you own a retail store specializing in Christmas gifts, develop a second line—such as picnic supplies—for summer months.

- **Be creative.** Look for innovative approaches to attract customers to your business in the off-season. For example, if you run a bed-and-breakfast in a summer tourist location, organize special events such as writers' conferences or knitting retreats to attract guests in winter months. If you run a nursery, conduct indoor-plant gardening classes to bring customers to your shop in February.

- **Offer off-season discounts.** In slow times, it's more important to have money coming in than to maintain large profit margins. Offer attractive discounts to customers who buy in the off-season. For instance, if you sell patio furniture, give customers deep winter discounts with the option of taking delivery in spring or summer.

■ **Stay in touch year-round.** Your customers don't vaporize during the off-season. Develop a mailing list of your high-season customers and create a monthly email newsletter. Keep your name in front of them so they remember you when they're ready to buy. And if yours is a summer-heavy business in a tourist area, now's the time to mail past customers "Welcome Back" discount coupons or offers.

■ **Work with others.** As a small business in a tourist location, it may be difficult to attract visitors on your own. But the community as a whole may be able to create off-season demand. Some ski resorts, for example, have developed summer downhill bicycling programs, bringing tourists back to the hotels and restaurants in their communities. Help your community find ways to attract off-season visitors.

Additionally, all businesses—but especially seasonal businesses—need some basic business practices to insulate them from the fickleness of seasonal finances:

■ **Manage your cash.** Small businesses live or die on cash, not profits. The single most important step for long-term survival of a seasonal business is managing cash flow. If summer is your high season, start setting aside a percent of income in a reserve account to use during winter.

■ **Get to know your banker.** Work on getting and keeping good credit, and establish a line-of-credit to call on in the off-season. Yes, you can use credit cards, and there are companies that will offer you sky-high interest rates once you're in trouble, but a solid line-of-credit with a reliable bank is your best bet. You've got to be able to pay your bills when the tourists leave.

■ **Keep off-season costs down.** In addition to managing your cash is managing your costs. During your slow season, reduce expenses as much as possible. If practical, employ workers on a seasonal rather than permanent basis.

■ **Prepare for your high season.** Use slower periods to get ready for the rush. Produce your goods or order inventory; make repairs or conduct maintenance on your facilities; train your employees in sales and customer service. Attend industry seminars to improve your skills.

NOW WHAT?!

92. Be the less expensive alternative

An old joke: A store owner purchases pencils for ten cents a piece from the manufacturer, then sells them to customers for a nickel. Noticing this bizarre behavior, his partner asks, "How do you expect us to stay in business that way?" The man replies, "Volume!"

Competing on price can be risky business. And in good economic times, competing on price is a particularly hazardous strategy for smaller businesses. While low prices may have led huge online companies and big box stores to grow, small businesses just can't manage the narrow profit margins of being a cut-price competitor.

But in bad economic times, customers are searching for lower cost alternatives to the products and services they buy. If you can find a way to be *the lower-cost alternative* (not necessarily *cheap*) for something customers already want and need, you can find a way to grow your business in a downturn.

How can a small company, which may not qualify for the supplier discounts or achieve the economies of scale of a larger business, become the less expensive alternative?

- **Work smarter.** Let's face it, a lot of your competition is either too slow, too big, too complacent to change. That gives you the opportunity to improve profits through innovative practices and by making your business leaner.

- **Utilize technology.** Technology can give you an edge, especially if your competitors are slow to embrace technological advances. There's a raft of "off the shelf" applications that can both improve your profit margins and increase customer engagement with you.

- **Focus on value, not price.** Value is a term used to mean the combination of price and quality (or convenience), and many customers look for good value, not just low price. When you shop for a winter coat, you may be willing to pay higher prices to get quality that will last many years. See how you can add value to your offerings if you're not able to lower prices.

■ **Build loyalty to you, not your price.** Even if you initially attract customers through introductory offers, sales, specials, or lower prices, work to develop the kind of relationship that keeps customers coming back even when the price goes up. A client may be willing to pay a higher price for your printing services if you can deliver the job faster with higher quality than your competition.

■ **Target the right customers**. Not all customers are willing to pay more even for better quality. You've got to make certain your marketing efforts are aimed at those who can appreciate the differences you offer. This doesn't just mean targeting upscale customers; there are value conscious, not just cost sensitive, customers at every income level. It means making certain your marketing materials focus on the other positive ways—not just price—that make you different from your competitors.

THE SH*T'S HIT THE FAN ...

NOW
WHAT?!

99 RECESSION-PROOF TIPS FOR
SMALL BUSINESS SUCCESS

GROW THE
POWER OF
SMALL
BUSINESS

What you need to know since the sh*t's hit the fan.

When the world came to a screeching halt because of Covid-19, small businesses were hit first and hit hardest. Businesses all along American Main Streets were shuttered, and huge online retailers and online grocers picked up the slack. Small retail businesses that sold books or clothes or household goods were required to be closed while huge big box stores that happened to also sell groceries could remain open. And politicians had no effective answers. Government aid was slow and bungled. Politicians of both parties—most who've never worked in a small business—had no idea how to address the real needs of real small businesses.

The bungled response to Covid-19 and the lack of effective help for small businesses proved one thing: Small businesses need to raise their own voices, become their own advocates. We can't depend on "business groups"—not even our industry associations—to advocate for us.

At the same time, it became apparent to more consumers that their favorite local businesses—their favorite coffee shop or restaurant, their favorite bookstore or sporting goods company—were threatened. There's rarely been a time when so many people understand the fragility of small businesses and are motivated to do something to help.

So now's the time for small businesses—and the self-employed—to come together, band together, and speak up to help all of us survive and thrive.

93. See yourself as part of a movement

Small businesses are an endangered species. It's time we all pull together to save this endangered species—which includes our own small companies. We need to see ourselves not just as individual businesses—often competing against each other—but as part of a movement, working together to help each other survive and thrive.

Movements have power: They help shape the national conversation and they help shape behavior. The environmental "movement" helped people think about their purchases and created pressure on companies to become more environmentally friendly in their purchases and behaviors. We all need to do our part to help our communities—our families, our friends, our neighbors—understand the importance of our movement: saving local businesses.

Look at an example of how pulling together, seeing one's own business as part of a movement, helped one small business sector survive: independent bookstores. Under the onslaught of a huge online bookseller, independent bookstores—"indies"—pulled together. Instead of seeing the independent bookstore across town as their competitor, they started to work together to help the local community understand the importance of local, independent bookstores.

So, as you think about yourself and your business, don't just think of what kind of business you have: You're not just a hairdresser, an app developer, a construction company. You're also part of a movement—the small business movement. Help build the power of a movement.

NOW WHAT?!

94. Understand the importance of small and local business

To help you as you advocate for small businesses, it's useful to have the facts of the real importance of small and local businesses to our economy and communities. There are 30 million small businesses and self-employed entrepreneurs, and they truly are the backbone—the spine—holding the American economy together.

Small businesses:

- Make up 99% of all companies in the US

- Employ nearly 50% of all private sector workers in the US

- Are responsible for over 40% of all private sector payroll dollars

- Create 65% of all net new jobs in the US

- Account for one-third of American exports

- Survive—about half of all new small businesses last five years or more

Purchases at local businesses contribute far more to local economies than purchases from chain or online companies—providing the critical tax dollars for schools, roads, fire and police departments, social services.

"Independent retailers return more than three times as much money per dollar of sales than chain competitors," according to the American Independent Business Alliance. On average—48% of every dollar spent at a local business stays local versus only 14% at a chain store.

The health of the American economy depends on small businesses, local businesses.

95. Buy local, buy small

Every time I see a neighbor receive a package from a huge internet retailer or grocer, my heart hurts a little. By ordering online from a big company, I know my neighbor has denied a local business or a small online business the chance to stay in business just a little bit longer.

Start with your own actions. Both in your personal life and in your business life, try to help a fellow small business owner out. Patronize the businesses in your own town. When looking online, see if you can first find local businesses, then check for small businesses.

Be willing to pay a little bit more, drive a little bit further, be a little bit more inconvenienced just so you can help the small companies in your community thrive. Think "Indies First" in all your purchases.

Does this mean you should never patronize a large business or one that isn't in your hometown? Of course not. Keep in mind:

- Franchises are often locally owned, especially restaurant and fast-food franchises. There's a good chance that behind the counter of that national chain, there's a small business owner and most of the money generated is going to stay right there in your community.

- Some big corporations really are on the side of small business. A few big corporations work hard to serve small businesses well, not just with competitive prices but with services truly designed for small businesses.

- You've got to do what's best for your own company. Some products or services are only available from large or non-local businesses or the price or quality difference is significant. Your first obligation is to ensure that your own small business survives.

96. Team up with other small businesses

There's power in numbers, so as you think of yourself as part of the small business movement, pull together with other small and local business owners to increase your power and amplify your voice.

There are many ways to do this—you can join other very local retailers through a Business Improvement District (BID). You can join local business organizations or local industry groups. You can join ethnic, gender, religious, or LGBQT entrepreneur groups. Join national organizations that advocate for creating a fairer playing field for small companies like yours, such as Main Street Alliance (www.mainstreetalliance.org), Small Business Majority (www.smallbusinessmajority.org), Small Business for America's Future (www.smallbusinessforamericasfuture.org).

And look for ways that local small businesses can pull together to provide services for each other. Many national platform companies—like food delivery services—often charge sky-high fees or take large percentages from small businesses. See if local companies, by working together, can find alternatives that keep more money in the cash registers of small business.

97. Support your employees

As was stated, small businesses employ nearly half of all private-sector workers in the US. Since we are BIG job creators, we also need to be GOOD job creators.

Small businesses often have difficulty recruiting top-notch employees. Employees often like the prestige that comes from working from a well-known company. And typically, those companies offer fairly good benefits (not always, of course—many large corporations are scrooge-like toward their employees). They also perceive big corporations—wrongly or rightly—as offering more job security and possibilities for advancement.

We all have a part in changing the perception of small businesses as a less-desirable place to work. We can do that by offering competitive salaries with decent benefits, including health care and retirement programs.

Often, of course, we can't afford the full range and quality of benefits of some large corporations, but we can offer a better workplace environment. It costs nothing to be a fair, caring, thoughtful employer—and that builds loyalty. Provide flexibility with scheduling—as much as possible—to meet the needs of your employees, so they know they are treated as full human beings and not just human *resources*. Give part-time workers set schedules so they can arrange childcare or take college courses or have another part-time job.

Be the kind of boss that gets your small business employees to say to others: "working for a small business is great."

NOW
WHAT?!

98. Vote

One of the most important things you can do to help your small business—and other small businesses—is to VOTE.

For far too long, politicians have taken small business owners and employees for granted. During an election, they may trot out an everyman small businessperson—a "Joe the plumber" or "Jill the hairdresser" to show they have small business supporters. But when it comes to actually passing policies and tax reforms that help the average Joe and Jill, not just their big donors, these politicians are nowhere to be found.

Don't be taken in by "pro-business" rhetoric. When most politicians talk about being pro-business, they aren't talking about YOU. "Pro-business" is usually shorthand for "pro-big business." When they boast about being anti-regulation or anti-red tape, politicians really mean "let the big guys get away with anything they want." And that's never good for small businesses.

We need policies and politicians who want to do more than just cut taxes and cut red tape; we need elected officials who will **even the playing field** for small companies—who will actually enact pro-SMALL business policies. Vote for politicians who will take on the big corporate special interests and have your small business back.

Your vote—as a small business owner—is critically important. And you need to become a *sophisticated* voter—not being taken in by simple chest-thumping by politicians touting how much they love small companies while doing the bidding of fat-cat lobbyists, billionaires, and big corporate interests. Don't just vote along old party lines—those labels don't necessarily mean what they used to.

Vote in every national election, state election, local election. Find out what's happening in your City Council, your State Legislature, who your Congressperson and Senator are. Vote for those who'll *truly* advocate for small and local companies. Make sure you vote!

99. Spread the small business word

We are all in the fight for the future of small business together, so raise your voice and your flag on behalf of the small business community. If you have a physical location, put signs up saying things like "Shop Local, Shop Small." Place similar messages throughout your online presence—your website, social media posts. Add the tagline to your signature on emails.

We are all part of a movement to save the small business sector. Our voices count. When talking with your friends and family, mention the importance of small and local businesses. Don't be a nag about it—but let them know how proud you are to own and run a small business and how important small businesses are to their communities.

Finally, always, always be proud of your own contribution as a small business owner. You create good new jobs. You support communities. You invent new products and services. You provide vitality and interest to your local area. You truly *are* the backbone of the American economy. And together, whatever the economy holds—good times or bad—we small business owners have the grit and the smarts and are willing to do the hard work to come out on the other side. We have what it takes not only to survive but to thrive.

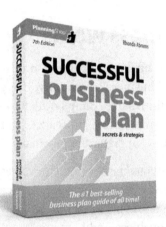

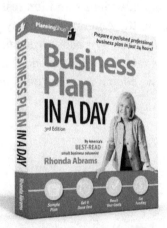